DEWSBURY MAN

Courting
1946 to 1992

Cliff Moiser (signature)

by
Cliff Moiser

British Library Cataloguing in Publication Data

Dewsbury Man: (Courting 1946 to 1992)

I. Title

ISBN 0 946873 14 3

First published in Great Britain 1997 by Basset Publications

Published by Basset Publications, Plymouth

Printed in Great Britain by
Peter Howell & Co.,
The Printing Press,
21 Clare Place,
Coxside,
Plymouth
PL4 0JW

For Christopher, Penelope and Robin

(Who are not *really* a source of great worry to me)

By the same author

Road Traffic Endorsements and Disqualifications – 9 editions
Practice and Procedure in Magistrates' Courts – 3 editions

•   •   •

Dewsbury Boy

Preface

The excuse for writing *Dewsbury Man* is that it was so much fun writing *Dewsbury Boy*, and brought about a reunion with so many old and dear friends, that I had to go on.

Additionally, I was under some pressure from former colleagues to "give it a go" about work in and around the courts.

I can only hope, as before, that readers get as much pleasure going over, to many, old ground, as I did remembering and recording.

It goes without saying, of course, that I need the money, ready for the millennium.

Cliff Moiser
Plymouth
September 1997

Contents

Chapter 1

The Apprenticeship

This was comparatively short for me. Five years at Dewsbury, three years at Buxton, three years at Coventry all as court assistant, rising to court clerk, and a couple of years in private practice at Leamington Spa.

Dewsbury, where I had grown up, as related in *Dewsbury Boy*, was typical of the times. A part-time justices' clerk who was only ever seen on court days, Tuesday and Thursday, and the Juvenile Court once a month, with just one full time assistant whom he paid from his salary for the job. There were about 1,200 justices' clerks in 1946, of whom 200 were full time, mostly in the cities and large conurbations, and 1,000 were part-time, usually one of the brighter solicitors in the small town or area. In 1992 there were about 250 full time justices' clerks, no part-timers, as all the smaller areas had been amalgamated with some others to create bigger empires. To me the loss of these part-timers was sad. They were so individually independent, and some whole time paid officials are not. They could tend to side with "the Establishment" however much they protested independence in public. I think also the part-timers were intellectually broader based, having to run additionally, often, a busy solicitors private practice. But once the civil servants (not any government methinks) decided on amalgamations, they followed as night follows day. It's a bit like police forces, really; if there are only 43 Chief Constables, they can be more easily controlled than 200. If there are only 250 justices' clerks, it is easier to manipulate them (I advisedly do not use the word control) than 1200. But that is how it was and is.

The court office at Dewsbury was in the Town Hall, outside the courtroom, and alongside, would you believe, the offices of the Chief Constable and deputy Chief Constable. It was a fine old fashioned office, with a high desk, along the whole of one wall, a loo annexed, and a coal fire. A policeman was supposed to replenish the coal from the cellars, but he was unenthusiastic, although I noted that the Chief Constable and deputy seemed warm enough in bleak winters.

Alas one window looked over the police yard below, wherein dogs were put down. It was an unhappy business as they were pushed into the wetted floor cabin and electrocuted. It was many years before the police offloaded that job to where it should have been anyway, the veterinary surgeons.

The court-room was beautiful old oak, with a large dock leading directly to cells below. It was a good place to learn, and one or two stories about the court appear in *Dewsbury Boy*.

I had a dog at this time, a cross bred black labrador called Basher. He was very faithful and walked with me to my office, maybe a mile, downhill. At the Post Office, opposite the Town Hall, I could tell him to go home, and very obediently, albeit reluctantly, he turned round, tail between his legs, and went home back up the hill – well he did for many months. And then, one day, after the usual routine of him turning round and setting off for home, I heard a scratching on the office door and there he was, tail wagging and a mischievous glint in his eye. I do not know to this day how he found me, as I think he had only been taken to the office once by me. A policeman told me later that the dog was sat patiently by the police swing doors, and shot through when the door was pushed open to let someone in – and headed straight to my office. I think he was known as my dog, so no one bothered. I was always glad that he did not bash on the Chief Constable's door. After that, he just came with me into the office, although he had to stay in the loo on busy court or office days. He was a clever fellow and when I used to sing about the house – for some reason I often did – he would put his head back and howl, joining in as I suppose he thought, the song and merrymaking. He was asleep in the loo at my office one day, when a little fellow was sent to an approved school (as they were then called) for some skulduggery and his mother had hysterics outside the office door. Poor Basher thought this great fun and howled and howled and howled. It was bedlam. She carried on hysterically, and he carried on howling and I couldn't stop him. It was all very sad, but I couldn't risk that again and he had to stay home thereafter. He did not like that, but there was much joy when I got home at 5pm.

Buxton was a similar, but smaller, set up to Dewsbury, a part time justices' clerk and just the one full time (80% full time anyway) court assistant. Except for the office accommodation which was appalling: dark dingy offices, and mine had a stone floor. The courtroom, such as it was, was in county property half a mile up the hill, far enough away for the justices' clerk to give the caretaker there £1, to use a county typewriter when needed for committals for trial.

The justices' clerk was also part-time Coroner and in those days before an Inquest, the Coroner had to view the body. One of the first I saw in that capacity was a tramp, found months after death in a hedge bottom, after the rats had been at it. Oh dear, a bit rough. These part-time jobs were quite profitable if you had enough of them, together with some property conveyancing and probates. Another offshoot was being clerk to the managers of a small country school, which I handled personally and kept the modest salary. I guess there were 20/30 pupils, and ordering the coke for the school boilers at five tons a time, loomed large in my workload.

Buxton is a delightful spot, a spa theoretically, but extremely cold at about 1200 feet above sea level. Winter woollies were a necessity. Even post Beeching, Buxton kept its railway largely to accommodate the professionals, including stockbrokers, who lived there and commuted to Manchester. There was a thriving rugby club and cricket team for which I played, and a theatre that became a leading emporium, still is I gather, in the North West. Being poor, I can recall paying one shilling a head on a Saturday to sit on the back row with very hard seats. Still it made it easier to stand up and yell out loud as I got cramp after a hard rugby match earlier in the day. My wife sat there, looking ashamed.

Derbyshire County Cricket Club had one county game at Buxton, a sloping field, but a good wicket. Bill Edrich, the England batsman was there for his county one year and I was appalled to see that he hadn't shaved for two or three days – he was in front of his time! I played for Buxton II on that ground, but with not much success, although I got the ball to move about a bit in the dampish atmosphere.

Coventry was my next port of call, being number four, a court clerk, in a hierarchy of 20 or so full time bodies all told. I reckon I learnt so much there under the wing of the justices' clerk, Alex Murdoch, (the Boss), and his deputy, Les Barlow. Alex Murdoch was one of the first clerks of a Metropolitan magistrates' court to come out into "the country". They multiplied later. Entry for the Metropolitan courts' clerkships was via the Civil Service examinations then, and there was no necessity to be a solicitor or barrister, indeed most were not. There was a good civic restaurant near the Coventry court where we had lunch. Fish and chips, bread and butter and tea were three shillings and terrific value. Us lesser mortals ate with the Boss, even occasionally with the Town Clerk. Several of us wanted tips on how to get promotion, so at lunch we asked the Boss how he got the job at Coventry. He said it was easy: everyone on the short-list, except him, had to give three months notice to leave, whilst he could leave the Metropolitan Court giving one month notice only. He was quite sincere that that had got him the job, but he was too modest. Being clerk at Bow Street during the war meant he was much involved with resident aliens, whether they posed a risk to the war effort and needed to be imprisoned, or whether they posed no risk and were allowed their freedom. There were some fascinating tales that we prised from him over our fish and chip lunches.

Coventry was and is cosmopolitan. 'Midst all the crime and unsavoury goings on in the city, I spent considerable time on domestic cases, where one or other of the parties lived elsewhere in the Commonwealth, Australia, Canada, West Indies, and so on. It seemed to me unreal, at that time, the mid fifties, that a woman here could get support money for a child (or herself), support from across the world. It was a lengthy affair (via the Foreign Office), but some could, and did. It was ironical that a father intent on non-payment of child support was better placed in Scotland than Montreal, although that situation soon changed.

Even local cases were not without interest. One single girl got an Affiliation Order against her single boy-friend, as he admitted paternity, and was quite happy to pay child support. But she had another child a year later, with the same father and result. And another six more children in virtually successive years, all with the same father and same result. The child support money had to be paid into court, and the girl became quite a favourite with the two ladies who ran the maintenance support office. So much so, that one of them ventured the suggestion that perhaps she should marry the fellow and save the annual case at court, "I could" the girl said, "but to tell you the truth, I don't fancy him".

They were happy days, not least for the court activities, as well as fish and chips. It was the time of Suez, and the Boss persuaded the authorities that he was self-employed, which very technically he was, and thus got a petrol allowance for his commuting. He had bought a cottage on the border of Northamptonshire, and needed petrol to commute. Actually he played on the true position, that a justices' clerk was not an employee (equals little or no petrol coupons), as all other staff downwards were. By statute he held an appointment, quite different.

At about the same time there was a rateable value change, and his cottage was assessed at the high figure of £9.00 per annum. This incensed him, being a Scot, and so he appealed and I believe he got it reduced to £8.00, or even £7.00. The rest of us had houses assessed at £30.00 to £40.00 per annum. Part of his evidence was the smallness of the garage, which necessitated the dangling of a tennis ball on a string from the roof, so that when the tennis ball touched the windscreen there was one inch from the front bumper to the rear wall. All good stuff, and good copy for the local newspapers who went to town on it.

After a few years at Coventry, I felt I needed "rounding off", and decided to have a spell in private practice. I had had quite a business whilst at Coventry, with full approval of the Boss, in conveyancing, as the builder of my own house at Cubbington, half way between Coventry and Leamington Spa, instructed me to sell his spec houses, and I mostly got instructions from his house buyers too. Quite lawful then but not now. I took these clients with me to Large and Major in Leamington Spa, and quickly gathered many more.

I took on some conveyancing work early on and enjoyed it. My builder friend bought up plots of land for eight or nine houses, which must have been profitable for all of us: it was for me.

Came the day when the Earl of Warwick needed to raise a few million pounds, and he sold off a few thousand acres by auction. My builder friend bought half a dozen plots. It was memorable for the root of title, a document or documents showing and proving owner-ship for the previous thirty years. The root of title here in the contract comprised words similar to this.

It shall be conclusively presumed that the Earl of Warwick owns Warwickshire.

Just that, take it or leave it. We took it. Came the completion day at the offices of the Earl's London solicitors, and maybe ten or fifteen of us buyers' solicitors drank the proffered coffee and fiddled with our Bankers' Drafts, but then the bad news. There had been frightful gales in the channel the previous night and all the ferries were port bound in France; the Earl was fast in Calais, and no, he had not signed the 50 or 60 conveyance deeds. Chaos reigned, and half the solicitors stamped off in high dudgeon. The rest of us handed over the Bankers Draft against the Earl's Solicitors undertaking to send on the signed deeds as soon as the Earl touched English soil. They did too, but it was quite exciting at the time.

I always found the affairs of the Earls of Warwick sad. I should have been unsympathetic as the proceeds appeared to go on riotous living, but I could not, as they, *seriatim*, sold everything. Warwick castle was sold in 1978, after 400 years in the family. The 9th Earl then sold off all the Van Dykes, the Canelettos and the Rubens.

Life got hectic. I soon had to drop the conveyancing as the criminal work expanded at a very rapid rate. The practice in Leamington had been part ecclesiastical, as David Major's father had been the Diocesan Registrar, and we quickly worked out it was not good tactics to have his old lady client from the church, in to make a codicil to her will (more to the church, and away from that naughty niece?) sitting in the waiting room next to my client, charged with rape, burglary, or robbery. We made separate waiting rooms, sharpish, after only a few months, and it worked.

I acted for quite a few villains in Leamington Spa, but soon I got instructions from Warwickshire Constabulary as well. I enjoyed all this change of scenery, and got round the local courts in Kenilworth, Warwick, Southam, Coventry and Stratford on Avon.

I was acting for a man accused of indecent assault on a male youngster, and with difficulty persuaded him to plead guilty in the Coventry magistrates' court, with a maximum sentence there of six months in the dungeons. Just before I set off for Coventry I got a telephone call from the court. It was the day that Archie Marshall was made a High Court judge, and he had to drop his cases immediately at Coventry Quarter Sessions where he was Recorder, but set about celebrations to which the boss was invited. The question was would I act as court clerk in court 2, if my indecent assault case was kept till last in court 1. I was bribed by a fee of five guineas, so I accepted with alacrity. Later, none·of us could remember a solicitor acting as court clerk and advocate at the same court, same day. Alas, the magistrates (at 1.00pm) in court 1 declined to accept our indecent assault case and the accused later got three years imprisonment at the Quarter Sessions.

I got another telephone call a few months later, this time from County Hall in Warwick, asking me if I would sit as clerk to the county Quarter Sessions, as there was a complex case involving the County Council and the Clerk of the Peace could not sit as he was also Clerk to the County Council. Five guineas was mentioned so I shot off on the appointed day. Again it was quite unusual, as the two jobs, justices' clerk and Clerk of the Peace are mutually exclusive. There was an unusual twist. I was invited to lunch with the judge in the members dining room – I remember a superb lunch – and I sat next to the then Lord Lieutenant, Lord Willoughby de Broke, who was intrigued to know that my grandmother had been his father's Nanny, before she emigrated to Yorkshire.

Mind you it wasn't all fun and games. My client was alleged, alas correctly, to have been quite beastly to a cat, as a result of which it nearly died. I got him to call at my office before court at Leamington, as I usually did with clients to check they were "soberly" dressed, and we walked to the court together. I should have known. There was a mass turnout of the Cat Lovers League, and we were hissed, violently, (I should have said there were cat-calls), for fully 50 yards until we got into the Town Hall. I always reckoned the crowd would have lynched him, if he had not received a short jail sentence, and my own safety was not certain.

I think the nearest I got to being thumped was at Leamington Court. I was prosecuting for Warwickshire Police against two ladies of mature years, who had the unfortunate habit of booking into many hotels in the Midlands, staying four or five days with the best of everything, champagne, the lot, but then leaving without paying the bill. You would have thought that butter wouldn't melt, etc., and they looked so respectable and refined. I had to oppose bail when I got them committed for trial – well there were 20 or more hotels involved, mostly 4 star – and I had to read out the older ladies' previous convictions which ran to three or four pages. It was unbelievable, there must have been 10 or more for fraud and many more for theft. She'd been married three times, once to a barrister, and had served a long prison sentence for fraud in Canada. The positioning at Leamington court was not good, the accused too near me, and as I got to page 2, I saw her, from the corner of my eye, clench her fist and pull it back ready to strike, but I sidestepped smartly to my right and her chance was gone. I had played rugby until about then, centre three-quarter and even though I say so myself, I had a neat side-step, which I put to full use, successfully. A close run thing.

Southam magistrates' court, sitting once a week, was one of my favourites. It was chaired by a Knight of the Shires, Sir Charles (I forget the surname) and he ruled with a rod of iron. On one of my first appearances I found the court was in the village hall, off the High Street. We pleaded guilty to a modest burglary (or theft) and I put up a far reaching mitigation, needed because of my clients' background of a liberal state education, approved school, detention centre, borstal and a couple of short imprisonment sentences. That was all in the past, I said, as indeed it was, but not that far past. But this woman had come into his life and they were shacked up (I didn't use those words) and she was pregnant. They would marry when both their divorces came through. She would keep him on the straight and narrow henceforth, and that would have been supported by every probation officer in Warwickshire, if there had been one there. My information was that probation officers were not allowed in that court. And then the job. It was true that he had not worked for some years but he could start on Monday, with a construction company owned by a friend. The company did not actually construct anything but was responsible for knocking down most of Birmingham City Centre, ready for rebuilding. I skipped lightly over the problem of getting from Southam to Birmingham, as he couldn't drive; he was disqualified for about the next five years. I sat down, exhausted, but almost believing what I'd said. The bench retired to consider, which was good, as normally they didn't bother. Alas back into court came Sir Charles and his team ten minutes later discounting my master effort and my client got six months imprisonment. Luckily I told him that he'd get that and he had his toothbrush with him.

But as Sir Charles intoned, "Six months imprisonment" I looked up and above his head was a large banner which said it all "A Happy Christmas to You All." The caretaker had forgotten to take it down from the Christmas Dance festivities the previous night.

There was a part-time justices' clerk at Southam, a most delightful man, and of many parts. You could get the most attractive insurance rates for buildings, contents, motor or life – by applying to the justices' clerks office, Southam. Thus said the Leamington Spa Courier. It was a bit near the mark.

I completed a house purchase at the office of the justices' clerk, in his capacity as a private practice solicitor, and it was a hot day. He sat there in shirt sleeves, and every single part of him showing, a lot, was covered in tattoos. He must have been ex Royal Navy but I never dared to ask. He was a good letter writer, and it was some years later that I heard of one of his better ones. A solicitor from Coventry appeared at Southam Court, and was a bit put out at the facilities which were nil – you had a conference with your client in a yard at the side of the village hall, and of toilets there were none for the public, although the magistrates could use the hall ones behind the Bench. The solicitor wrote to the Lord Chancellor's office to complain about all this, and the office in turn wrote to the justices' clerk asking for comment. The letter back came from the justices' clerk quite quickly, to this effect. There had been a court at Southam for several hundred years No-one had ever complained before. So far as the toilets were concerned, there was a yard at the side of the hall with a wall at the back and men had often used that. So far as women were concerned, they were simply expected to contain themselves. I did not dare ask what the follow-up to that was, but it must have been fascinating.

I prosecuted for the Royal Society for the Prevention of Cruelty to Animals and for the National Society for the Prevention of Cruelty to Children. I learnt a new court procedure at Stratford on Avon, prosecuting for the N.S.P.C.C. The Polish accused did not appear when his name was called, and I was about to ask, respectfully of course, for a warrant to arrest him and bring him before the court, but the justices' clerk beat me to it. He was a short tubby man, but he stood up with alacrity, and with outstretched arm, pointed at two policemen sat at the back of the court minding their own business, and said "Fetch him". This was most effective as it cut through red-tape and they shot out through the door, to return with the accused some 30 minutes, if that, later. I often wanted to use that procedure in later years when I was a justices' clerk, but search as I might, I could not find the authority to do it in Stone's Justices' Manual, or any other legal tome. When I later wrote a book on court procedure, I wanted to put that in but I was dissuaded by the publishers.

I must have been popular for some reason with local authorities as I was invited by Leamington Borough Council to prosecute for them. The very first case was against a local fruit and vegetable shop proprietor, some of whose wares were displayed in boxes outside the shop (à la Open All Hours) but on the pavement, and not up two or three feet on a platform. I never knew that was an offence, until I looked it up and it was pointed out to me discreetly that the *raison d'etre* for that bye-law was that dogs "did things" on ground floor produce. Oh heck. The offender was fined suitably and costs were awarded against him.

This was a thoroughly pleasant life, but I thought I had had enough on one day when I had cases in seven different courts. You could only survive by getting a clerk to sit in on the Quarter Sessions/ Assize cases till you got there. Arranging to be 1st on in court X, not before 12 noon at court Y, and in the pm courts at courts Z and A. I must say that in those more leisurely days (for some) court officials mostly co-operated, and went with it whenever possible.

Warwick Assize listed seven or eight guilty plea cases a day, and I once had a say, prosecuting or defending, in every case listed. It was time to renew refereeing in the magistrates' courts and I decided to make applications for jobs I fancied, as a justices' clerk. I think I applied for three, and met Joe Ingham (later justices' clerk for Smethwick) at short lists then on the justices' clerks trail. We thought that the first one was fixed, but we wagered 2/6d on who would first be appointed a justices' clerk.

Blow me, he was appointed justices' clerk within six months, and it cost me half-a-crown, as it then was. I never fancied Smethwick and did not apply but I liked the look of Dudley a few months later, so I applied and was appointed, in my early thirties. I know the salary was just under £2,000 a year and I thought I was rich beyond the dreams of avarice. I was, both from a money point of view, and from a "people" point of view.

Chapter 2

The System

I spent most of my working life as a justices' clerk, well over 30 years, and it is still surprising to me how little the general public knows of the duties and responsibilities of such an official.

The late Laurence Crossley, the justices' clerk at Uxbridge for many a year, used to tell the tale of the new telephonist in his office, who mistakenly put through two consecutive calls to him, when they should have been diverted elsewhere. Each caller identified Laurence as the justices' clerk himself. The first said "You're rubbish, I want to talk to the chap who actually fixes the court sentences" The second said "Ah, you're the chap I want to talk to, you're the fellow who tells the magistrates what sentence to pass". Laconically, Laurence used to say his job, in that respect, fell somewhere between the two views.

It is not surprising there is sometimes confusion in the public mind, as the system is not even clear what to call the justices' clerk. It could be the justices' clerk, and there is a Justices' Clerks' Society. But it might be clerk to the justices, clerk to the magistrates – there is a Magistrates' Association – magistrates' clerk or even clerk of a magistrates' court. Of course, justices' clerks get called other things, not always complimentary. Problem is almost all contested court cases have a winner and a loser as there are very few draws. So you start out with 50%, the losers, knowing full well you got it all wrong – usually again.

A justices' clerk has other duties thrust upon him with no choice. Clerk to the licensing committee, dealing with grants and refusals of pub licences, off licences, restaurant licences, and their frequent licensee changes. Late night drinking extensions, and licences to drink at the local gala, or other special events come within the purview.

Clerk to the Betting and Gaming Committee is another job. This deals with the licensing of gaming casinos, bingo halls, and bookmakers permits. Woe betide the justices' clerk who arranges for the annual renewal of bookmakers permits at 2.30pm on a day when there is racing at the local course. It used to be compulsory in the early days for a bookie to attend but I suspect that applications can now be made *in absentia*, unless there is some objection to the licence or renewal, but an 11am start of the court is a better bet. It was remarkable how many bookies paid the licence fee in fivers.

Secretary to the probation liaison committee is also compulsory though I fought a rear guard action to avoid it. It used to be called a probation case committee, and its job was to review (some, very few) probation cases with the relevant probation officer, and give him advice. It then became a liaison job as the probation officers said they did not need supervision of their handling of cases, certainly by magistrates. It was/is used as a means of putting forward propaganda to sentencers, magistrates and judges, to make them order more probation or community service, thus enlarging the probation empire. The justices' clerk was able to escape all this for years, as there was power to delegate the job to a probation officer, and then overnight, in the early eighties, without a word to anyone, the beastly Home Office made a regulation abolishing the right to delegate. Shame.

There are then a whole group of appointments where the justices' clerk might or might not be involved. And much depended on the court area, part of a shire county on the one hand, or a City/County Borough, later a metropolitan district, on the other. Some Cities (Plymouth) became part of the County, even though larger in population and area than some metropolitan districts. It was a crackpot system, no logic and no sense.

In the metropolitan districts the justices' clerk was automatically by law the clerk to the magistrates' courts committee. In the shire counties the committees could choose a justices' clerk, or otherwise. Otherwise was the clerk of the county council, an official whose knowledge of magistrates courts was nil, and that was where it all went wrong, as somewhere over half the shire counties chose the clerk of the county council, and the committee was treated as just another county council committee when that was the last thing that it was. In the Cities/ County Boroughs, then metropolitan districts, the magistrates chose a dozen or so members and that was it. In the counties each division had a minimum of one representative to this committee, and proportionately more for larger divisions. A division with six magistrates had one representative and a division with 139 magistrates had six representatives and this led to many county committees coming out at 30+, far too unwieldy. They came to some odd decisions.

Their duties, on the face of it, were quite responsible, being accountable for a budget of several million pounds. The appointment of justices' clerks, but only if the Home Secretary approved their choice. Even the Home Office wanted to guard against the sometimes bizarre appointments suggested by these committees. The committee could theoretically dismiss a justices' clerk, but in practice it was virtually impossible without Home Office approval, because of safeguards, except perhaps for dishonesty. The appointment of all staff to assist the justices' clerk, although whilst they could appoint, the staff worked under the sole direction of the justices' clerk. Luckily appointments of staff were delegated to the justices' clerk over the years. The committees' wings were clipped again, and they could not interfere in the day to day running of the magistrates' courts, although one or two tried to. The committee tried to fix a budget, after consulting the City/County Council, but often the County Council fixed the budget and that was that. Not so in the cities. This consultation was because of the total court budget, 80% was paid by the Home Office, and 20% by City/County Council. If you don't cry for Argentina, don't cry for the Home Office either, as its income from fines far exceeded what it paid out in court running costs.

If a budget could not be agreed, the Home Office arbitrated.

It was all weird and wonderful and it surprised any thinker that it worked at all, but it did in the Cities, but not in the Counties, where chaos often reigned. New court houses could be decided by those committees, but neither they, nor the councils, had any money and so the Home Office had to decide – merely to give the council permission to borrow the cash and pay it back over 40 years. The Home Office also determined how much cash could be borrowed.

Being involved in the building of two new court-houses I found the Home Office most helpful to justices' clerks, and the building department was about the only one that knew what it was doing, I often thought.

Computers needed approval by the Home Office to purchase, or lease, and this was a merry game. But first the magistrates' courts committee needed to approve computerisation. A serious suggestion was made in Devon that the computer should be based in a small town with about 200 cases a year and a court once a week, and not in the city with 5,000 cases a year, running six courts a day. We only got round it in the end when I refused point blank to touch it unless I got carte blanche to research the position, and order it myself, if appropriate, giving the committee a note of the cost only. We got the computer in a couple of years and all was well, but it was heavy going in the lead up to it, as the committee tried to renege on what it had agreed.

The overall position therefore was that the real power to spend was in the Home office, and not the magistrates' courts committee and it was a good job too. The magistrates' courts committee could refuse to sanction anything, so it was a negative position really. I gather things are better these days and one or two magistrates on the committees have some outside business experience. The committees are much reduced in size, to a dozen or so, and many county council clerks are giving their time to the county council, as justices' clerks take on the role of clerk, or chief executive as he is now called. But those large often unwieldy committees were responsible for some pretty dreadful decisions. On a bad day, in Devon I recall indicating to my own chairman of the Bench, that I really wouldn't allow the Devon county committee to decide where to buy the office tea, Tesco, the Co-op or Asda, as they really would have got that wrong. He was inclined to agree. The Lord Chancellor then took on the "control" of the magistrates' courts committees from the Home office, and things would have got better but for Government cash restraints post 1990.

It is difficult to see how the system has survived for forty years or more, especially with county council involvement, but it speaks volumes for justices' clerks and some magistrates, whose common sense made the unworkable work.

The Advisory Committee was possibly the most important of all the committees. The selection of new magistrates and the sacking of the very few bad eggs and poor attenders at court were the main tasks. In most of my time the names of members of the committee were not disclosed to the public, who could only be approached via the secretary, the justices' clerk, or the clerk of the county council in the blighted counties. It had been thought that they might be "got at" if their names were made public, and "nobbled" by those who sought appointment. But the names were made public in the late Eighties, and my information is that there are some cases of nobbling as some of us thought there would be. The committees comprised senior magistrates only, until a lay member was introduced at the same time. I could never see the point of a lay member, but some civil servant could and persuaded the Lord Chancellor to do it: I never saw the reason for it, other than it seemed a good idea at the time to others. There were no reasons of course. Interviewing candidates for the Bench became the norm, and it wasn't long before the civil servants created a form of how to interview, and then demanded two interviews. There was always a super abundance of lady candidates for the Bench, 40 something and children about to leave the nest. Men about 40 were the most difficult, as the private sector refused to give them time off for court (who can blame them?) so you were left with largely state employees, teachers, lecturers, government employees (or their wives) and so on. The public service employees had to be given 18 days a year off for public duties, with pay, so they were there. The Lord Chancellor put a limit on the "educators" at 15%, but it was sometimes honoured in the breach rather than in the observance.

Most justices' clerks became Training Officers for
Magistrates in the Sixties, a position of considerable
influence. From the year 1400, or thereabouts, until 1965
there was no formal instruction for newly appointed
magistrates whatsoever, they learnt from colleagues as
they went on, although a few of us had concocted three
or four informal sessions for new appointees. The Lord
Chancellor's office took the central role, and before long
it all got out of hand, as it would. The instruction was
divided into two, Stage 1 and Stage 2. There would have
been a Stage 3, except this was turned into "ongoing"
training, to be followed by Chairmanship training. All
this became Big Business, and compulsory, when all that
was really needed was a few informal chats, from time
to time, and sessions on new laws. Training is grossly
overworked as I see it.

It did allow Training Officers to get the Top Brass
before the magistrates though, and whilst the training
content from these VIP "lectures" was never high, it was
a good morale booster for the lay magistrates. I got the
Home Secretary (Leon Brittan) down to Plymouth; also
the Lord Chancellor (Lord Mackay – a fine and talented
man), the D.P.P. (Allen Green) before his downfall, the
Presidents of the Family Division of the High Court, Sir
John Arnold and later Sir Stephen Brown; and Lord
Denning, of course. There were quite a few more of
similar calibre. Training Officers were mostly quite
innovative, and some first class audio instruction tapes
were made, to be followed by some quality video tapes.

Training Officer for Court Staff was another appointment many of us held, but I found that easy. All I did
was create enthusiasm for practical and academic
learning, often by persuading the troops they were
capable of certain levels, as they were, when sometimes
they doubted themselves. But even that has now become
centralised, or regionalised anyway. I suspect the results
will be no better than the "old days".

Chapter 3

Dudley

Some friends thought I was mad, going to work in the "Black Country", after leafy Warwickshire. It is true that workmen and women made nails in the garden shed in years gone by, the slums were dreadful, and work in the steelworks heavy and dirty. Such was the heat and sweat loss that beer could be lawfully obtained almost any hour for the works to counteract the fluid loss. But that was years before my time, although the Road Oak steel works was still there, and Jim Barnsley still made the biggest and strongest chains in the world, many for use with anchors in the world's largest cruise, merchant and Royal Navy ships.

The bench at Dudley was best described as strong. No nonsense there. I only found out years later that after I was appointed justices' clerk, and before taking up the job, the deputy Chairman of the Bench, Dolly Chambers, took the Chairman of the Bench, Leonard Hillman, on one side and asked him if he thought they were right in appointing "that Mr. Moiser" as he was so young. The Chairman pondered a minute and then said he was sure, it was nothing a year or two would not put right. I was certainly the youngest justices' clerk in the Midlands, by years, but the age of appointments gradually came down in the next two decades and there are now quite a few justices' clerks who were appointed in their late twenties.

Leonard Hillman, the Chairman of the Bench for years, was quite a character, and was the managing director of a vast leather company. He was an Alderman and chairman of the Education Committee. I knew I had arrived when invited to lunch in his directors' room at the works. It virtually overlooked the local theatre on Castle Hill, and my predecessors for lunch had included Laurel and Hardy, Vesta Tilley, George Robey, Gracie Fields and almost every top artiste who appeared at that theatre, in the prime music hall days. Mr. Hillman collected jade, and when he died his home in Dudley was described as an "oasis" in the area, Dixon's Green, by some valuer in estate duty affairs. He was a great and popular chairman, who always gave "the young clerk" his head. He often said to me, "What do you want?" I said an extra typist, a new courthouse, or whatever. Inevitably he said "You shall have it."

He had one bad habit in court. I called on a shoplifting case (from Woolworths) in my early days, and heard a commotion behind me, and much garbled talk. I thought I was being attacked from behind. What in fact happened was that the chairman said, in one word "GotsharesinWoolworthscan'tsit" and shot off for an early lunch, scrambling round or over any unfortunate magistrate on his right. I soon learned and kept Woolworths cases to the end of the list, just to keep him. The Hillmans holidayed in Montreux mostly, and his doctor was known to be flown out when necessary. He asked me if we would holiday in Montreux one year. He was way out: I was working out if I could afford a caravan at Caernarvon.

Dolly Chambers, the deputy chairman, was also a great character. Her husband had lent George Wigg £50 to help him become Labour MP for Dudley (and he paid it back) in 1945, I think it was. She was a Governor of Dudley Girls High School, and accepted their invitation to go with the girls on their summer cruise, about 1965 it was. An insurance man called on her at home and demanded an extra £2 because she was over 70, and the risks were greater. She refused to pay and after much haggling she intimated that if the man kept on she would take her mother with her on the cruise. There was no answer to that. She never paid the £2! Her mother was indeed alive and about 103. Dolly herself lived to be over 100, and I know one son, the City Treasurer of Gloucester, had retired normally before she died. Her other son was multi-lingual and worked as a senior interpreter for the United Nations.

I think possibly my favourite magistrate was Cliff Whitehouse, also a Borough Alderman and Chairman of the Borough Finance Committee, a difficult job even in those days. He ran his own coal factor business. He used to breeze into court at the last minute and always, but always, said he would have to resign the Bench, he couldn't do that and the finance committee, t'was too much. I worked out an answer. I said I had fixed it that he was sitting with me in court 2, and it should only last an hour and a bit, as I was tight for time too, and court 1 was an all day job. It worked and I kept him to the end. The end, yes. The retiring age for the Bench then was 75, and it was the custom for kind words to be said in open court on the retirees last day. The sitting chairman indicated the retirement, and said what a good chap the outgoing fellow was, served the area well, for 30 (or whatever) years, great feel for justice, yet humane, kind, and of sound judgement. Occasionally of course these words were true. In any event the justices' clerk asked to be associated with the kind words, and there was further support from the senior solicitor present, the senior policeman there, often the deputy Chief Constable, and in a moment of weakness I had agreed the senior probation officer might muscle in on the fond farewell. It all took 20 minutes.

Cliff took me on one side one day after a short court 2, and said he was 75 in a couple of months time. I said I knew and I was sorry to lose him. I was too. He said he did not want any ceremony in court to mark his retirement. I asked why as the other Bench members would wish it, and he said, he had a slight stutter, "Wwwell. It will be rrrreported in the local pppaper, and my yyyyoung llady friend wwwill then know my aaage. I dddon't wwwant that." I'll say this; if he'd told her he was only 60, (and he probably did) she would have believed him, as that was all he looked. There was no ceremony.

Cliff Whitehouse, Alan Young, Luing Preedy and a few others had dinner together two or three times a year. A very convivial evening and great company. They asked me to join them one day and I said I really couldn't. The previous week I had been out every night, dinners, training sessions, cricket nets or whatever. On the Saturday morning, at breakfast, my wife actually introduced me to our children, and all three (the youngest was about 5), stood up, shook hands across the table, and said "Very pleased to meet you, sir." I suspect that they were primed. But I explained this to Cliff so he could see how serious it all was. He said "Gosh, you're lucky". I couldn't see it at all, until he said "It would have been really serious if the children had said they thought it was the fellow who came round on Thursdays, when you were always out."

When I first got to Dudley I had to see the Bank Manager. He asked me what I thought of the locals, and I said that many had been very kind to me as the new boy. "Yes" he said, "I've found that", – he was fairly new too – "But they won't sign anything. However if they say the money will be repaid on the 1st March, it always is, on the dot." And so I found it. There was much honesty by the villains even, and pleas of Guilty more prevalent than other places. In fact, I made a bit of a name for myself suggesting a not guilty plea be entered occasionally, and I was often right, which surprised me.

I was approached by one villain (the first of the Teddy Boys) who was appearing at the Quarter Sessions, and he asked me whether to plead guilty to a section 47 assault, or a section 20 wounding, and he knew the maximum sentences were about the same. I said he should do what his lawyers advised, as I had gone to some trouble to get him legal aid, not automatic or freely given in those days. He made my day. "They don't know much" he said, "I want to know what you'd do." He pleaded guilty to the section 47. Another villain used to write to me from Dartmoor and I suspect that I was the only person who answered him. He was quite concerned about his list of previous convictions, which he thought was wrong. The list comprised about 108, mostly for drunkenness, assault, theft and so on over thirty years or more. He was sure that it was only 101 or thereabouts, so I did check the queried ones against the court register from time to time and we corresponded.

The option to plead guilty by letter to minor cases came into operation in my time, and much fun was had by all. Some gems came in. "I plead guilty to parking on double yellow lines. I have just come out of Winson Green prison, serving seven years, and no one told me about double yellow lines on my pre-release courses." Another, " I thought if I got my nearside wheels inside the yellow lines, but off the pavement, I would be in order." Fined £1 each, the mitigations simply deserved it. All these possible guilty by letter cases were listed for afternoon courts, in batches of 50 or 60 at a time, to avoid cluttering up the morning crime courts. The police had long since given up even attempting to serve these summonses personally, so these "shorties" were sent by recorded delivery post. All went well for some time and then there was a postal strike, lasting several weeks. No summonses went out, and the cases dried up quickly. What to do in the afternoons then? As I realised that we would get hammered when the strike was over (we did), I thought a little relaxation might be in order. The morning courts carried on as normal, but come lunch time we set off to tour the nearby racecourses, leaving two or three in the office to hold the fort. Perhaps four or five of us got into the largest car and we visited Wolverhampton, Ludlow, Uttoxeter, Worcester, Stratford-on-Avon, Warwick and several others. Eric Gregory, my then deputy and friend, had never been to a racecourse in his life, and was very impressed. At Wolverhampton, his first visit, he kept winning small amounts on the first three or four races, and I asked what he had backed in the penultimate race. Shyly, he said some rank outsider at over 20 to 1. I rubbished this as throwing his previous winnings away. "Not a chance," I said. I stood a furlong from the winning post and watched his choice almost walk home, the nearest rival being some two hundred yards behind. Beginners luck, but it did him no good as we made him buy us all a steak lunch the next day.

George Marlow was a lively character on the Bench; he was twice mayor of Dudley and later became mayor of Bridgnorth, a bit unique. He managed a rather nice hotel in Bridgnorth. He didn't drive, so as I lived in Bridgnorth I took him into Dudley on his court day, though he had to wait for me in the afternoon, unless I could use him in pm courts as well as am. He was chairman of court 2 one day, and the whole list collapsed, as they do, and as I popped into court to see how they were getting on, I found the place deserted at 11.30am, except for George reading the office copy of the *Times*. I wasn't in court as court 1 had a long committal for trial case which was more in the deputy's line than mine. George looked up from the *Times* and said "There's racing at Ludlow". I got the message. I rushed up to my office and made sure my desk was reasonably clear, and off we went. We backed the winners or places in the first five races, and would have won the last had the horse not fallen at the last fence fully 50 yards in front of his nearest rival. We had a delightful afternoon tea between races. From the winnings I even bought my wife chocolates. We arrived back at the hotel in Bridgnorth about 6.00pm, and I was invited in for tea. Mary, his wife, rushed to get us tea and sticky buns and remarked that we must have had a hard day. "No, no" I was about to say, "We've been racing at Ludlow", but George gave me one of those looks across the teacups and I remained silent, as the P in Psmith. To this day I think Mary thinks we were flogging it out in court for hours on some frightful domestic case.

It was not all apple pie and cream (or beer and skittles) though. I wakened up one morning and heard on the radio there had been serious rioting in Dudley the night before and over 50 men had been arrested and would appear in court that day charged with, mostly, public disorder offences. I hastened through the cornflakes, and when I got to the office, true enough a long list of overnight arrest cases was coming in. There were over 50. There had been trouble between a coloured youth, with a knife, and a white youth, and then the whole thing went to a full blown riot, blacks v. whites. It was not long after the Notting Hill race riots, where sentences of five years imprisonment or more were handed down. Luckily the police only charged summary public order offences, so I got the deputy to take the normal courts in court 2, and I sat with magistrates called in specially in court 1. Cliff Whitehouse was chairman for several days. We sat 10.00am to 7.00pm and managed to deal with 25 or so, all guilty pleas. That left 25 for the next day and we duly started at 10.00am. But, in the meantime another 25 cases came in from the previous night as rioting continued. The second day we got through twenty or so cases, but retired about 7.00pm with still 20 or so left over, again for a day.

I can remember being quite concerned at a position where men were being arrested at a rate faster than we could deal with them, but it eased off on the third night, with only a handful of arrests, and a week later the town was as normal as it could be, as were the court lists. Inquests began. The police told me afterwards that the court sentencing had played a large part in quietening things down. The word had got round that anyone convicted of any disorder offence was being sentenced to imprisonment, (which was true) albeit often only one month, and no more than six months (for bad assaults). It was the immediacy of the sentencing that was crucial, and the Notting Hill sentences of five and six years were not really needed, and certainly no more effective than imprisonment for a few months, imposed next day, or the day after that. This was obviously before probation reports were made virtually compulsory, causing delay, and thank goodness for that. The court won widespread praise from the ordinary citizens of Dudley, and whilst violence simmered under the surface, black v. white, it never broke out again on the scale of that week. Sitting through all those cases left me horror struck at man's inhumanity to man, and the hate released into violence.

The Home Office telephoned me half way through the week to commiserate and ask if there was anything they could do. It was nice of them and unexpected but there was nothing. Trevor Cropper (Wolverhampton) came across and acted as clerk in a couple of "orthodox" pre-fixed courts, releasing me for the "riot" courts, and the coroner lent me his court, (next door) for the orthodox. It taught me that you need some sort of emergency plan for occasions like this and I had one thereafter. The need seems not to be there today, legal aid abounding and there for the asking, and bail adjournments there freely available; probation reports are "compulsory" and take three weeks to prepare and whilst it all may be desirable (I doubt it) this has taken away the immediate sentencing impact. As I write the Home Secretary has plans for speeding up cases for juveniles, but he has lost as the damage has been done, mostly by his and previous governments, and is probably irreversible.

I was lucky throughout my professional life that the local detectives were always good to excellent. At Dudley the local detective chief inspector was a dour Scot, and I swear he actually knew a crime was to be committed before it happened. I only ever once saw him disconcerted. I had a habit, approved by the Bench, of course, when the police did not object to bail on a remand, to say to the police prosecutor, "Whilst you do not, the court might, tell us more" And occasionally the accused was kept in custody until the next hearing. These were always quite serious cases and not minor trivia. This put paid to some cosy deal between the police and the villains. "Admit this burglary and I will not oppose bail in court".

A man was charged with the theft of some very valuable Brierley Crystal, £20,000 worth, or more, from a local public building. The night before his court appearance, the detective inspector telephoned me and said that he was not opposing bail, and there were reasons which he did not want to disclose in public: would I not open up bail or custody as I sometimes did. The reason was that a detective sergeant from the Fine Arts Squad of the Metropolitan Police had been up and spoken to the accused. If out on bail, the accused would lead the Met. to recover some very valuable paintings and other *objets d'art* in the London area. I kept quiet and bail was granted. On the return date the accused did not appear to face trial, and I was in a "I told you so" mood. Alas, a few days later the detective inspector telephoned again with the news that the accused *and* the Metropolitan detective sergeant were in custody in London, accused of conspiracy to steal valuable paintings et al. – no, no property whatsoever had been recovered. The detective inspector was not best pleased. But he had to accept it with such fortitude as he could muster.

I had the view that many Dudley criminals were honest in the way that they pleaded guilty when caught. That is not to say that they were not devious. They worked the system. The Recorder of Dudley, Gilbert Griffiths, was a fearsome sentencer on his day, and was feared certainly by local burglars. Five years imprisonment for house burglary was not unusual. On the other hand the Recorder of Wolverhampton was a real softie, and suffered badly from probationitis. The local burglars knew when the Dudley police were about to pounce, after a period of active burglary. So, one or two went across the boundary and committed a burglary in Wolverhampton, leaving fingerprints. In due course they appeared at Wolverhampton Quarter Sessions and pleaded guilty. Ten or twenty cases in Dudley were "taken into account", and probation ensued, thus five years imprisonment was further delayed. The police had told me this and I was sceptical, but a couple of burglars confirmed to me that they had actually practised this system to good effect.

It was Gilbert Griffiths who sentenced my Dartmoor correspondent to three years imprisonment. Whereupon the offender, on leaving for the cells, turned to the Recorder and said "You Bastard". "Bring him back", said Gilbert. The prison officers did. "I got that wrong" said Gilbert, I meant to say Five years". The pure Appeal Court reduced the sentence to three years, on the basis that derogatory remarks by a prisoner should mostly be ignored.

I think one of the nicest men I ever knew was Percy Wadsworth, the Town Clerk of Dudley, a real gentleman: and he was also clerk of the Quarter Sessions Court. He and Joe Harrison, the Borough Treasurer, were a formidable team, and both could have achieved much higher status had they wanted to. I remarked to Joe Harrison, (another Yorkshireman) one day, that I was surprised at the number of Yorkshiremen in senior positions in the area. "Oh," he said, "that is easily explained. "We get the jobs the Scots don't want."

I never met Ernie Brown, the part-time justices' clerk for Tipton, who went just before I got to Dudley, but he was characteristic of the area, with dozens of part-time justices' clerks around. He was against women, and women court attenders were made to sit on one side of the courtroom, men on the other side. All women, young and old were called "Ma". As more women were appointed to the Bench they too were made to sit on the women's side on the Bench. I often wondered how he would have coped with women's libbers two decades on.

One of the best old style policemen in Dudley was given the task of finding and getting convicted a man who would insist on urinating through shop letter boxes in the High Street, or nearby. He didn't have much luck on his stint of night duty, but code-named the perpetrator as the "Phantom Pisser". But he got someone on his next night shift, caught him, he did, coming out of a shop doorway fastening up his trouser front, and yes, there was urine inside the shop by the letter box, and none in the shop doorway. The man's version of affairs was, well, garbled, partly because he'd had a few beers, putting it mildly. He pleaded not guilty at court and to everyone's amazement was acquitted. The police officer was not amused at all. The Chairman was of the naive opinion no human being could stoop so low, like that, the basis of the decision. Unfortunately he indicated that openly. Actually the perpetrator did not need to stoop: he chose letter boxes half way up the door. Alas, the Chairman himself ran a clothing shop only a 100 yards or so from the court, and near the High Street, and would you believe within two weeks, someone had urinated one night through his shop letter box. The old style police officer was on duty that night, but as he said, he had worked his beat slowly, thinking these things didn't happen as the court said. He had passed the chairman's shop about midnight .... The Phantom Pisser then seemed to fade away.

Dudley was, and is, a wonderful place, and the first "big event" for me was the West Midlands Order 1965, which created five large county boroughs, Dudley, Walsall, Warley, West Bromwich and Wolverhampton, each serving a population of 200,000 or more, with a common police force. The district councils around the five towns had fought desperate rear-guard actions to prevent it, but to no avail. Dudley was joined by Brierley Hill, and parts of Sedgeley and Coseley, most members of those Benches joining the Dudley Bench. They didn't like it, but the Chairman and I went out of our way to make sure, somehow, that the Chairmen of these Benches, and their committees, were at least deputy chairmen of the larger body and its committees. I think it was 1967 before I got the first acknowledgement (from Brierley Hill I remember) that the new arrangements were better, in that they sat in a very impressive court room now (they did) not annexed to a police station, and the central heating was better than the coal fire in Brierley Hill courtroom. They could park their cars more easily, but the real glory was tea (and the occasional biscuit) half way through the morning, which they had never had before. I reckon that clinched success, and I never thereafter neglected the provision of tea. A winner.

The administrative work in creating the new Boroughs was enormous, as pubs and off-licences had to be divided up from previous registers. We certainly granted extra drinking hours to the rugby club, and then found out it was just outside the boundary. The greyhound stadium was just inside, but another court gave them extra drinking. But it all settled down very quickly, albeit Trevor Cropper at Wolverhampton said he would never go through that again, and would resign first. The five justices' clerks, with Tony Darbey, the Clerk to the South Staffordshire Stipendiary Magistrate (a quite anomalous affair) held monthly or bi-monthly meetings to try to come up with common policies to help the new West Midlands police force, and had some successes. We had lunch as a break on these days, as the meetings started at 10am. There was an occasion when we were still on item 1 on the agenda at 7.30pm, but that was a one off. We must have had one Society dinner with wives, because they met. They were complaining to each other about arrivals home at midnight, and beyond, on days of Five Clerks meetings. Betty Ingham asked my wife if she could stop me keeping Joe out late, and mine replied that I said that it was Joe who kept me out late. We were rumbled. Betty indicated that she got a new electric washer as compensation for late nights. My wife indicated that she got a box of After-Eight mints – and that I had eaten most of them anyway. It's the way it was.

Life continued pleasantly, until the government of the day, about 1970, decided to re-organise the centuries old Quarter Sessions and Assize courts around the country; these courts were quite efficient in the midlands with part-time judges, and part-time court staff, but elsewhere, particularly in London, all was not well with long delays for hearings, and some poor court administration. So there was born the Crown Court, inflicted on all, good or bad. With bigger administrative staff (of course), full time too, and away went hundreds of years of history with the abolition of Quarter Sessions and Assizes.

The short term disaster was that the Act gave immediate and absolute priority to the Crown Courts for court accommodation, and the poor relations, the magistrates' courts, were pushed out from their court rooms where they had sat for years. Long term though most areas got new courts, but it took so long. In the meantime temporary accommodation had to be found. We found an unused falling down library in Dudley, only 200 yards from the High Street, and we quickly, within three – four months, adapted it, bought a large Portacabin for two courts and moved in. It was unusual but adequate for a few years. The one real drawback was that we were only a few hundred yards from a very old pub which still brewed its own beer and on Mondays, brewing day, with the wind from the East, we got the full blast of brewing hops, not a pretty smell, although the end product was well worth the investment of a few pounds from time to time. I invested. Two of the girls in the court office were physically sick at the brewing smell, but life went on and things could only get better.

There was no trouble at all to resolve that we needed a new courthouse, and the Home Office agreed. There was a very good site available half way between the old courthouse and the temporary one, again only two hundred yards from the High Street, and five minutes walk from the bus station. On only a slight slope, and space for court car parks, with other free parking nearby.

I used to worry that, whilst the job was satisfying, and was of some use in helping to keep some semblance of law and order around, I never did anything creative. Planning a new courthouse soon put an end to that. I was lucky having extremely helpful architects, but you had to brief them clearly on what you wanted. There were hundreds of dilemmas, one being, in a two storey building, whether the court rooms were on the first floor and the offices down: or the court rooms on the ground floor and the offices up: or, botched job(?), some courts up and some offices up, with some courts down and some offices down. I tackled that by carrying out a survey to see how many people attended court, and how many merely attended the offices, over several weeks. By a margin of about two to one, more people attended the offices. So the plans, finalised before I left, had courts up, offices down. On arriving at Plymouth, I carried out exactly the same survey, and got exactly the opposite result: by two to one, or thereabouts, more people attending the courts than the offices. So the courts there were down, and the offices on the first floor. I found the Home Office, whose approval was needed for the plans and expenditure, most helpful, but they slowed down the operation. The architect and I never attended the Home Office without coming away with a list of further problems to solve. I often found I got my own way in the Home Office by using bad language, but I needed new tactics when the Home Office court building Supremo became a lady. I think I solved that one by gin. The Home Office had no comment whatsoever on the planned office for the justices' clerk, which had, one way, a very pleasant view across Dudley Zoo, to the (ruined) castle on top of the hill. Oliver Cromwell must have been just about on the court site as his cannons let loose on Dudley Castle. The other, side view, looked out on very pleasant gardens and a bit of green space behind the High Street. The actual building was about to start shortly after I left, but I was lucky enough to be invited back for the official opening of the courts by Lord Widgery, then Lord Chief Justice. It was a very happy day, and we had a slap up dinner that evening. The Lord Chief Justice and I congratulated Dudley on their new courts. I found it very nostalgic going back and quite emotional, so many friends there. I probably made an undistinguished speech, but I recall telling the diners about the one and only time I ever heard the deputy justices' clerk, Eric Gregory swear. It was the day Barbara Castle imposed a 70 miles per hour speed limit on motorways. Eric was, and is, a BMW-Alfa Romeo-Lotus Elan man, and one could but sympathise with him, as I did from the seat of my Ford Popular, later turned into Ford Escort and then a Cortina at Eric's insistence.

It was a joke in my family for years that I would be the justices' clerk for Plymouth, as Paris was not available. I fell in love with Plymouth in World War II, saw it devastated and burning, and it was my Royal Marines base whenever I came back from abroad. I was demobbed from there. We visited occasionally as a family post war and saw it being rebuilt, slowly but surely. I had decided I needed a move, as I walked into my office, under the clock tower, every day and thought I just couldn't do that every day for another 25 years. And then Edward Foulkes, the justices' clerk for Plymouth, decided to retire after over 20 years there, at exactly the right time for me. It was unlikely I would be appointed there, so I thought. But have a go I must. It would be sad to leave Dudley, so many friends, but if not Plymouth, then somewhere else.

If I could secure the appointment, Plymouth or even elsewhere, several things would happen. – Not least, whenever I had an article published in a legal journal criticising, gently, or even bitterly, the Government/

Home Office for its latest outrage, John Jenkins (Tredegar) would be stopped from alleging it was yet another verbal "assault with a Dudley weapon".

In all my time in Dudley, I played cricket at Claverley, a delightful ground surrounded by trees on the outskirts of the village. They say that cricket stopped in 1940, when the pavilion was occupied by the Home Guard. Cricket recommenced in 1946, and the tea and coffee in the pavilion kitchen cupboard were exactly as left in 1940. Over the years, the cricket varied from ordinary village cricket to that verging on Minor Counties. There was an annual fixture against Glamorgan, due, I think, to friendship between the sometime captain of Claverley, Edgar Davies, and Wilf Wooller.

They were happy days and I can remember winning the 2nd XI bowling cup when I was 40. Some of the Dudley magistrates used to view the games, and picnic there. I was quite startled one day, early on, after surviving a loud LBW appeal to hear a loud voice from a boundary deckchair "Not out, yes, but put him on probation." My old friend Arthur Silcox, in good voice as ever.

I was captain of the midweek side for a few years, and persuaded some top class players to guest. Jack Flavell turned out shortly after retiring from Worcester and England, and there were several top Birmingham League players. Tom Roberts, a real Blackcountry man, was always available. It was said that he had a perfect arrangement with his wife, that he played cricket Saturday, Sunday and Wednesday, and other days when asked, and she ran the several shops he owned – although he did sign all the cheques. He played cricket until he was about 77 methinks, and still got a few wickets and runs.

There were scurrilous rumours about Wednesday courts at Dudley in the Summer. Not guilty pleas not allowed, court ending at 1pm whatever the state of play. All untrue, of course. However, I have to admit that court personnel were, what shall I say, involved a bit in the cricket. I was captain of the Claverley side, as I said: Arthur Silcox, Chairman of the Wednesday Bench, and Bill Guest, a court usher were willing hands as scorers. Peter Mucklow, waiting to go to Oxford, and later a solicitor in Worcester, who had opened for Shrewsbury School, was a temporary court assistant, and needed to open the Claverley batting, but that was all, well nearly all.

Godfrey Booth, a farmer, was on the way out as I arrived. The prankster. He saw a Claverley lady, the wife of a friend, at the bus stop in Wolverhampton one day, and immediately went down on his knees in the street in front of the entire queue, "Please come home, don't leave us, the kids need you." It caused havoc as the waiting passengers began to take sides.

He went fishing with a couple of team mates when rain stopped cricket. His friends asked how he caught fish when they didn't, and he explained that his brother was a pathologist and he gave him human flesh to use as bait. They didn't believe him until next time and he pulled out what looked like human flesh – in reality a pigs part trotter. One of the fishermen fainted.

The biggest hoax was him seeing a ghost in Bridgnorth church at midnight. It made national news, and the church was visited by all, but all, the Societies into the supernatural. He ran it for fully a month before confessing it was a hoax.

My last night in Dudley was great fun. My family had gone on ahead to pastures (and schools) new, so I spent the evening with the Detective Sergeant, visiting many of the pubs in and across the High Street, frequented by the local villains. I could have had 18 to 20 pints bought for me in those pubs that night, but I contented myself with four or five – something like that. I was surprised at the number of beer swilling customers who knew I was going, and their good wishes were a bit overwhelming. I should have known that never again could I be as close to the "criminals" as I was there. Partly because in bigger courts it is simply not possible, and in any case the job of a justices' clerk was changing from being in court daily to becoming a manager, with only the occasional appearances in court, doing the real job.

Chapter 4

Plymouth

Nearly all justices' clerks' appointments were preceded then by public national advertisement, short lists and interview, and Plymouth followed that line. Plymouth was popular as it had everything, its own magistrates' courts committee, Advisory Committee for selection of justices; it was a licensing planning area, and not least a population of over 250,000 putting it in one of the then higher salary brackets. The short list for interview was strong, really because of the presence of David Kidner (Cambridgeshire and later Coventry) and Roger Rickard (Colchester). The others were no slouches either. But the three of us worked out the appointment was between us, provided it was decided on merit, and correct form, and made some deals. Whoever got the job could use the (only available) telephone first to tell a wife. Whoever got the job paid for the dinner for the other two, as we three were booked on the sleeper train to London at midnight. We met the magistrates to socialise a bit for coffee and lunch before the interviews, and maybe we were all a bit nervous. David Kidner said he couldn't stand coffee without sugar, but he'd had three cups between 10.30 and 11.00am.

I was lucky enough to get the job, and then the deals came into play. They stood back to let me telephone home first. My wife "knew" I would be appointed, intuition of some sort, so I only said "start packing", whereupon she burst into tears, quickly converted to the joyous excitement of the move. She later said that to her, coming to Plymouth was just like "coming home" – that from a Yorkshire lass too. Then the dinner which the three of us had at the Mayflower Hotel overlooking Plymouth Sound. It cost me dear. It was a happy evening, and it was said I only just got to the sleeper in time, as I was at the wrong end of the platform waving a bottle of Beaujolais about, just before midnight. Possibly a slanderous statement that, but I do remember a slight headache as I got out from my cabin bunk at Paddington next morning. I called, bleary eyed, at my Dudley office on the way home to Bridgnorth, and I was only there half an hour or so. The first congratulatory call was from Frank Howarth (Birmingham) and later to become one of the first six court administrators for the Crown Courts. I could not understand how he knew, but news of the appointment was in the *Birmingham Mail* that morning, unknown to me. As well as giving congratulations, he said he was somewhat jealous, as in WW2, he was a second-lieutenant in charge of an anti-aircraft gun with a crew of six on Drakes Island, in the Sound, and became a lover of Plymouth, like me. There were many more calls similarly. It was great fun.

One of the very first social invitations I got was to a cocktail party in the Commando Forces, Royal Marines

Officers' Mess at Stonehouse Barracks, where I have since been a member for many years. It took me back in time, and after the party, wobbling slightly, I took my wife to see the bullet marks on the wall, but alas they were gone, worn away by time. Although they were there in 1946 when I left the Royal Marines at Stonehouse. One evening in the early part of 1943, I had gone out of the rear entrance of the barracks and into the Longroom for a work-out in the gym there, and was on my way back, just into the rear entrance, when I heard an aeroplane, very low, and if I thought anything of it, it would be of a Sunderland Sea 'plane, based at Mountbatten in the Sound, coming in to base. It was no such thing, it was a German 'plane which machine gunned, and as the bullets hit the wall five yards to my right, I threw myself into the hedgerow on my left. I moved faster then than I had ever moved in my life before, though I may have moved faster in later years. As I brought some of the hedge down, I realised with horror it belonged the R.S.M. (Ashby) who lived in the cottage there and so I never confessed to him that I was the culprit of his damaged hedge. I got back to my barrack room, albeit shaken, and told my new R.M. cronies that a deliberate attempt had been made on my life by the Luftwaffe, and they must have found out that I (and some of them) had decided to join the battle against them, fatal for them, of course. It was either Eddie Hughes or Phil Nuttal, who pointed out cold bloodedly, that on the other side of that wall (then) was Millbay Dock, (now the home of Brittany Ferries) wherein lay two or three merchant ships and they were the likely target, not me. This explanation quite spoiled my evening, and I sulked all night.

Firmly ensconced in Plymouth, I suddenly found myself with opportunities on radio and television, mostly at the BBC. I had only once appeared on television in the midlands, relating some of the events in the American courts. The scope was much wider in the South West, usually about crime and punishment, but other things too. I enjoyed "Any Questions", usually with the Trade Union Man, the Bishop, the C.B.I. Man and me. Early on I was first to answer a question from a leggy female teenager, with prominent teeth, sat in the front row. "In view of the rapid rate of inflation, if you have any money, should you save it or spend it?" The programmes were always spontaneous, and live which I preferred. I quickly guessed, rightly, the others would advise caution, the Trade Union Man would blame the government, the Bishop would pray for guidance, and the C.B.I. man would advocate a course of action which could be construed as spend *or* save. So I opted for some money to be spent in antiques, then a racehorse or two, (a tax saving gimmick at the time) but otherwise, spend, spend, spend, on pleasure. George Yandell (Nottingham) had, I think still has, a cottage at Salcombe in Devon, and he relates how he had driven down for the weekend, and switched the television on as soon as he arrived. He was met by my face, full frontal, and the end punch line, "So if you have any money I say Spend, Spend, Spend." George, apparently, turned ashen faced at this and said to his wife Dennie, "Oh dear, what have we done – we've just made him treasurer of the Justices' Clerks' Society, and he's a wild spender." He recovered though. George had strong views on spending, salaries and the like. He coined the phrase (about salaries when there was much talk but no money) that "soft words butter no parsnips", a phrase unknown to some justices' clerks, who thereafter called him the Parsnip Man.

I found the fishing cases most exhilarating and certainly in the early seventies, I managed to sit as clerk in court in all of them. The fines for the owners and/or skippers of foreign vessels fishing in "our" waters were enormous, and sometimes the catch was forfeited too. Maybe a few hundredweights: or maybe several tons, worth £10,000 or more. Lord Elwyn Jones, the Lord Chancellor, at one dinner asked me how the fines were going in these cases, and I said quite well. We had fined a Spaniard £25,000 the day before. "Not enough" said he, "we put the maximum at £50,000 to be used." I tried to explain that the Spaniard was a Basque, whose father and grandfather had fished there, or nearby anyway, for a hundred years, and under the new system no government in Madrid was going to give any licence to fish to a Basque. Forfeited catches were sometimes quite difficult. If the fish was rotting, no one wanted it: if it was refrigerated there was a possible market, low prices only if it was not edible and going only for fishmeal. We solved it in the end by a court decision. "The forfeited catch shall be sold, or otherwise disposed of, as the justices' clerk in his absolute discretion sees fit." It saved me some haggling on the fish market next morning, because I eventually gave the foreign owners first refusal to buy, at just under market value (or what Ag. and Fish and I thought was market value) and this saved offloading the catch, a costly business. I only remember once, when a catch was not sold, but taken to sea and dumped overboard, a whole days work.

The Royal Navy, as ever, were brilliant in their handling of these cases, and boarding the fishing boats in a choppy sea was no easy job. There were a few fishery protection vessels, usually a lot smaller than any frigate, and constantly at sea waiting to swoop. I used to wonder why the arrested foreign boat was brought into Plymouth, as any coastal court had jurisdiction. I knew I was popular with the Admiral, because if the Royal Navy, or Ag. and Fish, told me an arrested boat was on the way in, and they did mostly, and the likely charge was fishing in "our" area, wrong sized nets, wrong fish in the nets, or fiddled log book, or whatever, I arranged a court for 10.00am. next morning. Other courts would not or could not do this. My system pleased the Admiral because his fishery protection vessel could get back out to sea on the job within a day or so. He didn't have limitless resources. I was told later that I was not unpopular with the foreign captains (some of them owners) because, if the boat was worth £½ million, but the bank was owed £¼ million on it, there was no profit being tied up in harbour and court, and money to pay the mortgage was got by fishing again as soon as possible. Alas, I suspect that Plymouth was used for none of those reasons, but because, in a run ashore for the Royal Navy crew, even for a few hours,

Plymouth had Diamond Lil's Bar in Union Street, the then in-place, and no other South West ports had fleshpots anywhere near as exotic as this League I establishment.

There were some hiccups early on. We got a whisper up the grapevine that a court in Scotland decreed that the skipper should be kept in prison until the large fine had been paid. Error. The company owning the boat merely flew out another skipper, who sailed the offending boat into the sunset, leaving the original skipper stewing in the local dungeons for three or four months, and the fine unpaid. In the next case and thereafter Plymouth courts used the sentence "foreign boat to be detained up to three months or until the fine be paid", where it was mostly possible. But how to detain: the Act was silent. Unless some restraint could be used, the skipper could just sail off, leaving the fine unpaid. I explained the dilemma to the Admirals' legal adviser, Lt. Commander Louis Armstrong, himself now an Admiral in fact, after discounting my own staff's view to send a diver down and wrap a chain round his propeller, expensive, or take away his sparking plug – he had spares. The upshot was we had a meeting in the wardroom of the fishery protection vessel, suggested by the Royal Navy. This was attended by the Admirals' legal adviser, the Harbourmaster, and a representative from Ag. and Fish, Ministry of Defence Police, local police, plus the Ships' captain and Executive officer and me. It was not a big wardroom, It was "squashy", and I was breathing in as I was elected chairman, and never got chance to resist on breathing out. But we made progress.

The Harbourmaster, entering into the spirit of things, said he could and would direct the offending boat into the inner harbour – he has God-like powers – and this reduced the sailing time to two 2 hour periods a day, when the inner harbour gates were open. For those four hours, the M.O.D. police said they would provide a man on the jetty, with orders to jump aboard if the foreign boat attempted to sail off. Unfortunately we never got beyond that stage, because the ships captain got his Exec. officer to get the gin out, so we could all have a snorter. Well it was the Royal Navy, it was near lunch time, and they have this reputation for hospitality. We sort of never resumed, as a party developed, and it must have been my fault as chairman. I often wondered what further instructions could have been given to the unfortunate policeman for the period after he jumped aboard: would he end up in Vigo, Santander or Bilbao? Or a body washed up on the French Coast?

But the problem never arose, as the fines were paid that evening, and the boat sailed off lawfully. And, of course, we had provided a base for similar future activity if need arose, although it didn't. Apart from the fate of the policeman sailing off to the blue yonder.

It is another story about how the Royal Navy knew where to look for possible foreign fishing offenders. Ag. and Fish had a deal with the Royal Air Force, and paid for R.A.F. Nimrods to patrol "the box" between Southern Ireland, France and England/South Wales, reporting back possible offenders. This suited the R.A.F. well, as they got flying time at another departments expense. I think Ag. and Fish paid £10,000 an hour, it was something like that. This of course, with my enquiring mind, I had to see at first hand, and I went on more than one patrol. The first time I duly reported to R.A.F. St. Mawgan in Cornwall, the night before and had a fairly abstemious evening. No drinkee before flying, but I think I got the Air Vice Marshal's room overnight. A big, big breakfast at 8am, and the Nimrod was airborne by 9. Exhilarating.

My first shock was to find the pilot was not the captain of the aircraft. It would not have done for the "dam busters". The pilot was just the driver, and the captain sat behind him, in the well, in front of an enormous radar screen. The pilots were all graded, some were allowed to fly as low as 300 feet above sea level, and the most highly qualified at 250 feet. I can tell you that at those levels it was decidedly bumpy. A couple of Members of Parliament had been before me and were so ill they had to be taken back to St. Mawgan, to prevent death! But my time in the Barents Sea in WW2 stood me in good stead. I think the worst moment was when the captain spotted on the radar a possible offender immediately astern, and the aircraft turned 180° at some 400 feet. My stomach seemed to be elsewhere.

There was a crew of 8 or 9, all seasoned personnel, and included two photographers. At 400 feet they photographed all suspected boats, and the end result showed the number of the fishing boat, whether or not its nets were out, time and location fix. This was transmitted to Ag. and Fish and onwards to the Royal Navy and was quite brilliant, and carried out with the utmost precision. It was time for lunch after three or four photographs, and I gave a hand taking round the main course, fruit and coffee to the pilot, captain and others. It was unanimously agreed by the entire crew that I would have been accepted easily in the R.A.F. as a steward, if not chief steward.

Each patrol lasted some 10 hours and we touched down at St. Mawgan about 7pm, where there was a short debriefing, and then we could drink in our flying clothes in the officers mess "Scruff's bar", until we changed for dinner. We made up for the previous nights abstemious behaviour, as the crew had at least 48 hours free from further flying. In the bar I can remember the conversation often turned to pay, and how poor it was, (mine and theirs). The pilots, working for a commercial airline would get about double their R.A.F. pay, but their pay did rise substantially some short time later, I am pleased to say. They deserved it. Those Nimrod patrols carried on for some years, but eventually Ag. and Fish could not, or would not, pay up and thus ended an era of fishery protection. Ag and Fish were reduced to a small two/three seater spotter 'plane which I think still survives.

With the Courts Act giving Crown Courts absolute priority over court accommodation, the search for temporary courts was on before I even got to Plymouth. Taff Williams, the deputy at Plymouth, used to telephone me in Bridgnorth most mornings in the Summer of 1971, about 8.00am when I was scarcely awake. We trawled through various possibilities, disused schools, vacant garages (truly) and so on. We settled on the vacant

Officers' mess at Plumer Barracks, some four miles North
of the sea front, in extremely spacious grounds. It was
adapted to our modest specifications in about ten weeks,
a brilliant effort by the City Council workmen. We got
six courts, stacks of ancillary offices (I got the colonels'
room) and parking galore. We got daffodils in the Spring
and blackberries by the bucketful in late Summer; well
those the ushers left for us. We also got a gymnasium for
a year or so, until it was demolished, and we played 5-a-
side football every lunch hour. This compensated for our
loss of a swimming perk in the City Centre where we
had become friendly with the Holiday Inn staff, and used
their pool, certainly weekly. I had about three months in
what was shared accommodation with the Quarter
Sessions and County Court, newly built in 1965 or
thereabouts. I thought it was badly designed and was
quite pleased to move to Plumer Barracks, as I also
thought that shared accommodation never worked. But
Plumer Barracks was temporary, and we needed new
courts, which we got. The City Council had agreed new
courts and wanted to site them adjoining a new police
station, near the Plumer Barracks site. I suspect that the
magistrates had not been consulted. I had seen wet
bedraggled court attenders as they plodded in from the
nearest 'bus stop, and that would not do. Not everyone
has a motor car.

Another site was available, just South of Royal
Parade, and a hundred yards or so from the Crown Court,
City Hall and bus stops. It was a very run down area
with a garage and an ice factory on most of it, but due

for demolition. It was a small site, but in the right place and we grabbed it.

Tony Irish was an Architect employed by Plymouth City Council. He was assigned the job of designing the court, so we liaised and went through the new court saga. My experience at Dudley was good as I knew the Home Office people already. Tony said I gave him the best brief he ever had, and we never had a wrong word between us in the three year planning. His employers were not too pleased because we became firm friends. The work was made easy when Bryan Briggs was assigned as quantity Surveyor, and the three of us made all the decisions, so if it was a disaster, the blame was quite clearly on us. We were lucky in that Devon County Council had so many problems, taking in Plymouth, Exeter and Torbay in 1974, that it scarcely knew we were building a court (until we wanted a cheque for it) and we had nil interference from anybody.

It was finished in 1979, two months ahead of schedule, and about £20,000 cheaper than the estimates. Tony Irish got several architectural awards, as he had blended the building stone superbly with the surrounding Prysten House, St. Andrews Church and Elizabethan House. But it was more than just that. Everyone around started tarting up their buildings, and even gardens with trees and shrubs appeared. It became and is an attractive area.

Not everything was perfect, and we must have made some mistakes, but it was 90% right, and we suffered because the Home Office started sending officials from dozens of other courts, contemplating new ones, to view for ideas, and this was extremely time consuming for staff and for me: a full day sometimes. Even Jersey sent a deputation to view, and we turned that into a civic lunch day courtesy of the Lord Mayor. It was all very rewarding, but hard work on top of the daily grind of ever increasing criminal activity coming before the courts.

I used to be asked how you start building a new court and I simplified the answer. You get a blank sheet of paper and in the middle draw a box. This is where you make the tea. Just fit everything else around it. And so it was in fact.

The Prince of Wales came along officially to open the new building and we had a good day. A couple of years after I retired a disgruntled motorist drove his car up the disabled ramp through the plate glass doors into the court foyer. His point was as the court had taken away his money and his licence, it might as well have his car. It was a bit over the top, and would not have been allowed in my day.....

I was sat in the office one day, minding my own business, when out of the blue I got a telephone call from Michael Argyle, then sitting at the Old Bailey. "I've just had a telephone call," said he, "From Princess (I forget which one) in Monaco." This should have fazed me, but it didn't, he moved in those circles. "She asked me what sentence should be passed on an offender who had poured petrol over a cat, lit it, and burned the poor animal to death. I told her I'd never dealt with such cases as the

Bailey usually had higher profile cases, but that you would know. What's the going rate?" By chance, I had just been sitting as a Stipendiary at Bow Street, and elsewhere with a couple of cruelty cases. I needed to know whether it was my sentence he needed, or a lay magistrates' sentence. "Both", he said. I was by nature a bit hard, so my sentence was two months imprisonment, slightly more if the offender had any record of human or animal violence. A bit more difficult was the lay magistrates' one as it was borderline, stiff fine, or short imprisonment, depending upon the exact constitution of the Bench. A couple of good Conservative and/or Labour ladies was imprisonment: one or two wet male educators or somesuch would come out as a fine. He thanked me and passed on the message. The actual sentence in Monaco was two months imprisonment.

Michael had for many years enjoyed the Dublin Horse Show, but the I.R.A. got active, and judges had to notify the Lord Chancellor's office of their holiday destinations. He did and got a visit from security, who virtually forbade Dublin. In vain did he say he'd been there for the last twenty years, and they indicated that they didn't give a damn if he was kidnapped and tortured or killed, but the government of the day insisted on a no risk at all approach. I had just got back from America as this drama unfolded, and I proudly showed him my gambling winnings from Las Vegas, about $15.00, mostly from slot machines. So he went to Las Vegas instead of Dublin, but when he got back, he proudly showed me his winnings, a roll of $20.00 bills, a profit of several hundred dollars. Huh.

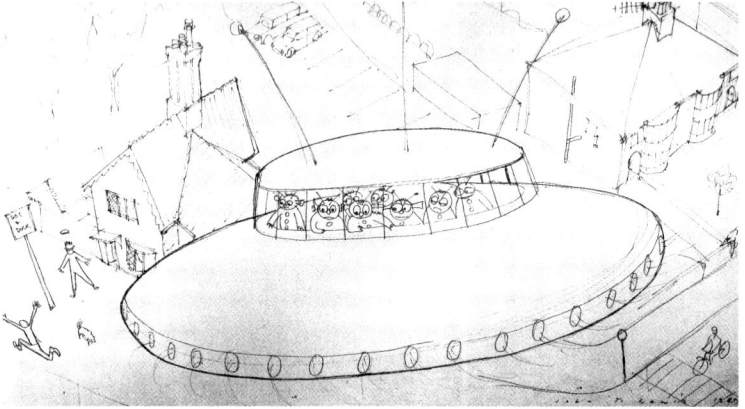

Martians in Dudley 1967.
Pictures recently released under 30 year rule.

Beauty in the dock.
Setting up temporary court. Dudley 1971.

Sir Niall Campbell (Barnstaple) the author, and
Sir John Arnold, President of the Family Division of the High
Court. Testing the equipment in the execution shed at
Devonport Dockyard.

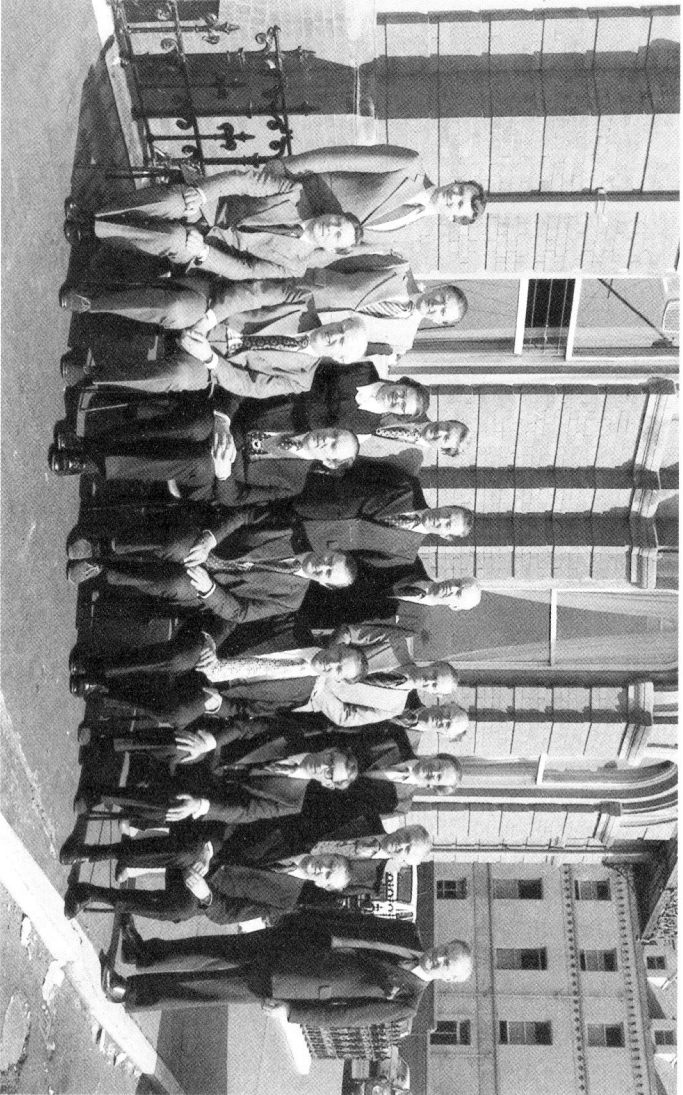

Council of the Justices' Clerks' Society, 1977.

"Topping out" ceremony at the new courthouse, Plymouth, and presentation to the author of the "silver spade",1979.

Opening of the new court at Plymouth, by H.R.H. the Prince of Wales, 1979. He laughed a lot then.

New court at Plymouth, 1979.

The pub, outside the front door, was for the convenience of the author.

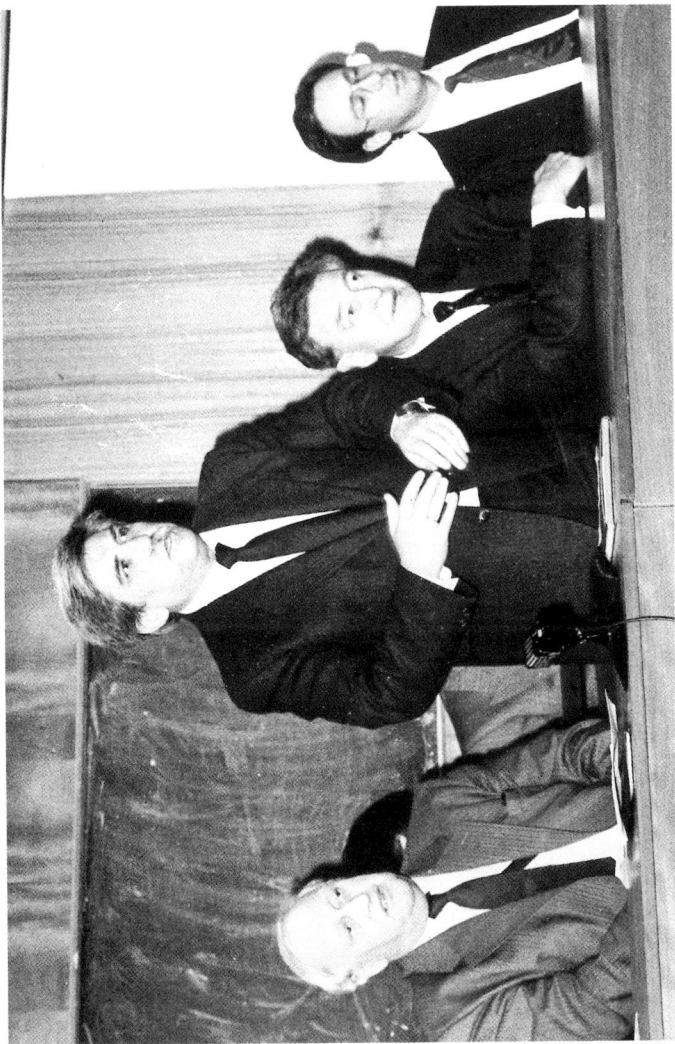

The author; Dr. Lev Khaldeev, Eric Crowther and David Tonner: Addressing Russian Judges in Moscow, 1989.

Chapter 5

The Justices' Clerks'
Society (JCS)

The affairs of the justices' clerks in England and Wales are controlled nationally by an elected Council, of the Justices' Clerks' Society (JCS), then of 15 members (now rather less) and three officers. All the members and officers were justices' clerks with full time jobs. So whatever effort was put into looking after the interests of the body of justices' clerks came from their own free time. This was a considerable load on the shoulders of the members, but almost unbearable for the secretary and the chairmen of the four or five committees into which the council was divided. How the society came up repeatedly with secretaries of the quality of Edgar Bradley (Poole), David Kidner (Coventry) and Gerry Sullivan (Bristol) was one of the wonders of the world. Their predecessors and successors were no slouches either. Cometh the hour, cometh the man, I reckon.

I was elected to the Council of the Justices' Clerks' Society in 1969 at Eastbourne, along with Roger Rickard (Colchester). In those days the number of votes cast for candidates was not disclosed, but it was leaked to me that Roger and I had obtained more votes than anyone else ever previously. It was good for the ego, until you got to the first quarterly meeting when the latest entry had to serve the tea and you were brought down to earth with a bang: it was also intimated that newcomers were not expected to speak much, if at all, for the first year or more as their views were of little consequence. And so it was.

There was much talent within the Council but it was often wasted. Some brilliant papers were produced on technical legal problems of the day, and I actually thought the Home Office read them, but it was years later that I realised the Home Office read them and applauded only when the conclusions actually coincided with the Home Office views. If they did not they were ignored. Much of the work was a waste of time in effect. But the meetings were congenial, mostly in London hotels, and I learned much in the bars of those hotels.

Bar discussions ranged far and wide, I suppose mostly about the failings of the last Criminal Justice Act, or Road Traffic Act, and how to put matters right in the next (imminent, always imminent) Criminal Justice Bill, or Road Traffic Bill. The only time there was real excitement was when the law changed on the first day of the month, and we found out, by a copy of the Act, on the 15th day of the month. That really got justices' clerks going. But there was a more worldly philosophical debate on occasions in the bar. For example, why God had placed the sexual channel, so near the urinary channel, in a mans' sexual organ. We never got to any definite conclusion on that as I recall. Or if Southend pier were

just over three miles long, and there was a bar at the far
end, just outside the three mile limit, would it require a
liquor licence? We were hopelessly divided over whether
it should be made a criminal offence to slurp your soup,
as was rumoured to be the case in Jersey. I have to say I
was strongly against criminalisation as I am a pretty good
soup slurper. I get this from my father, also good at it,
but he blamed his false teeth. We talked always until the
small hours, and it was John Brooke-Taylor
(Northampton) who promulgated the view that when I
went to bed, everyone went to bed. It was John, and he
could shift a pint or two and actually lived in a
"decommissioned" pub, who declared I drank a lot. He
was wrong, I had my half dozen gin and tonics like
everyone else, but then reverted to tonic only, and he
thought it was always gin. That's my story and I am
sticking with it.

Of course, I have nothing against alcoholic beverages,
in fact I am in favour of them. It is the fresh air that causes
most of the problems, not booze, as propounded by my
friend Mike Craig, (we went to the same school), a former
script writer or producer for Morecambe and Wise, Ken
Dodd, Mike Yarwood and many others, but a comedian
in his own right. He proves the point by recounting a
night out with three cronies, Bert, Sam and Fred in Leeds.
Several hostelries were visited and they ended up in the
Conservative Club. All was fine in the club, the
conversation was animated, but restrained (it *was* a
Conservative club after all) but when they hit the fresh
air at about 2am Bert was soon flat out on his stomach

on the pavement, at right angles to the road, and with his fingers over the kerb stone, shouting "Help me, help me, I can't hang on much longer." Sam was knocking on a lamp post, saying "Let me in, let me in, I know you're in I can see a light up there." Fred was sat on the kerbside, looking at the Town Hall clock, and muttering "Oh heck, I've lost two stones in weight in 12 hours." Mike couldn't help them as he was trying to light a cigarette from a Belisha Beacon, complaining it wouldn't stay on long enough. But it does all show the effects of fresh air.

It was Fred of course, about that time, who telephoned Alcoholics Anonymous one evening, "Yes" said A.A., "Thank you for calling, do you wish to join?" "No" said Fred, "I've pheletoned to shubmit my reshignation."

JCS Annual Conferences were much fun, but never without drama. In London one year, one member died in his hotel room. Another year, a chandelier in a lounge fell smack in the middle of a group of justices' clerks discussing, I think, jurisprudence, just missing several of them.

In Bath, where we were split between three hotels, several of us arrived back at the hotel at 2am, to find the place locked up. We had been told that there was always someone on duty, and there was, but he was old and deaf and couldn't hear the night bell. In any event he had gone off to collect the shoes left outside the bedrooms for cleaning, – it was one of those hotels. Some bright spark noticed a part open basement window, and I got half way through and was pushed from behind, unnecessarily I thought, to fall on the kitchen sink, full of unwashed pots and pans, and left over peas, potatoes and cabbage. It was not a pretty sight, and I considered shoving off to clean up, and bed, leaving the other bounders outside, but *noblesse oblige* came into it, and I went upstairs and round to the front door to let them in. The night porter arrived at the same time, well he would.

There was another successful conference at Harrogate, but the choice one night of after dinner speaker, a Lord Justice of Appeal methinks, and the topic, jurisprudence, were not to me wildly exciting. I have a liking for old time Music Hall as seen on T.V., and I thought I might eat early, cut the jurisprudence, and hurtle down to Leeds, to the City of Varieties, which I had not visited since my youth, and just get there for the opening at 8.00pm. I happened to mention this to another fairly new justices' clerk from Cambridgeshire, now a Circuit Judge, and he had similar views to mine, so off we both shot. We just made it for 8pm, hurriedly paid our £2 entry, and were met by the opening music. As Act I started, (we had no programmes as we were late) it dawned on me this was not Music Hall: it dawned on my colleague too. It was a strip show at Division I, with a bit of singing, but not much. For some reason we did not consider leaving, probably because we had been parted from £2, and the alternative was jurisprudence. When we left, two hours later, my colleague thought that the coloured girl, second from the left in the back row of the chorus had the biggest bosom he had ever seen, but I don't think he'd seen many. Big, yes, but not the biggest.

In due course I became the Chairman of the Parliamentary Committee, where it was obviously thought I could do least damage. The job consisted of perusing some Parliamentary bills, mostly Criminal Justice Bills, but it was pretty hopeless suggesting much, as bills that finally reached the statute book were nothing like the bill that was introduced at second reading. It really needed constant attendance at the House during Committee stage, and no justices' clerk could afford the time, and the Council could not possibly afford to fund it.

A former chairman did see a copy of a Finance Bill, some 150 clauses, and 30 or 40 schedules and missed a bit tucked away in an obscure schedule (it would have been a miracle if he had spotted it) whereby any justices' clerk who omitted to tell the Customs and Excise about the grant of a new pub licence committed an offence and was liable to a fine of £5. This had incensed some senior members of the Council, properly so, but it took several years to get it revoked.

Every paper submitted by the Society to central government, started with a paragraph 1 similar to this (now updated),

"The Justices' Clerks' Society, founded in 1839 and incorporated in 1903, is a professional body representing the principal legal advisers to lay magistrates in England and Wales. The justices' clerk is professionally responsible for advising the magistrates on the law, practice and procedure of the court, and for some of the training of magistrates: he or she has a duty to ensure that magistrates are advised by

assistants who are qualified legally and administratively to undertake those duties. The society is organised into regional branches and is controlled by a council of elected members. It thus represents a combined experience of magistrates' courts and their problems covering the whole of England and Wales. The Society does not limit its activities to promoting the interests of its members and one of its main objects is to keep under review the operation of the law, especially the law administered by magistrates' courts in England and Wales, to point out its defects and to support and promote proposals for improvement.

Public Service Role

The Society is consulted on a wide range of subject matters by Government departments, agencies and other professional bodies. Through a system of committees and networks, the Society is organised to respond to consultative documents, to review law, practice and procedure, and to make proposals for reform."

In my second or third year I was invited to draft a paper, giving JCS suggestions for improving road traffic law. The invitation obviously slipped through in a tea break. But, I thought, My Big Chance. I laboured. In due course, in the fullness of time, I circulated my efforts to other members, and it was discussed in Council – I have to say that, it was discussed, briefly. I cannot now remember all the clauses but there were eight or nine (I was restrained). The paper suggested the abolition of road tax with the equivalent tax being added to petrol tax at 5p or 6p a gallon. No fault insurance for traffic damage, to save enormous costs of private insurance and expensive often pointless litigation. To display an insurance cover disc on the windscreen, replacing the tax disc: and several other ideas of equally high quality. I advisedly stopped short of the death penalty for a third offence of illegal parking.

But then, lead by the cavalry (see below) every single clause, one by one, was demolished and I remember thinking I was lucky to keep paragraph 1, which was all that was left, plus one other.

I had one near success only, in years, and it again concerned road traffic. In 1971 or 1972 the Labour Government introduced a Road Traffic Bill, which proposed, amongst many other things, the total abolition of imprisonment, as a possible sentence for all, but all, traffic offences, including drunk driving, driving whilst disqualified and all the fraud offences with traffic documents. The Council agreed a list of 12 offences which ought to have the possibility of a prison sentence retained, and my job was to persuade government, who didn't want to know, to do just that. Some chance. I got one or two Members of Parliament interested, and got to Westminster to explain to a few MPs why total abolition was wrong. The meeting was chaired by Alan Clark, then MP for Plymouth Sutton, and I had just got under way, and was waxing eloquent when a head appeared around the door. The body with it then appeared and it was Marcus Fox, later Sir Marcus, the MP for Shipley, then a junior whip for the Conservative opposition. We had been at school together, as I mentioned in *Dewsbury Boy*. The conversation went something like this.

"Hi, Cliff, long time no see"

"Aye, didn't expect to see you here today"

"Cliff, the Government has just indicated that it is going to the country, but it wants the largely un-controversial Traffic Bill through. What about this imprisonment business?"

"Well, I have a list of 12 where imprisonment should remain"

"It is not possible. I've agreed with the government to keep imprisonment for four. Give me the four you want."

"Oh, well. Driving under the influence; driving with excess alcohol in the blood; driving whilst disqualified; and attempting them."

"Right, thanks. Goodbye." Exit.

It was all over in two – three minutes and it is the only time I saw Alan Clark's lower jaw sagging without any riposte. The meeting ended sharpish. It was only going home on the train that it occurred to me it was a rum way to run Parliament and make laws. And then I realised that I had forgotten "Refusing/failing to give a blood sample", which had always had the same maximum (imprisonment) sentence as the substantive offence of driving with excessive alcohol in the blood. It was too late and the *Times* later reported the four for which imprisonment was kept, and it was confirmed when I got my copy of the then Road Traffic Act. I pointed out my error but it still took over two years to get that put right in a later Road Traffic Act.

It wasn't all serious though. Pyramid selling bothered governments, as it was thought to be almost fraudulent. I wrote around the Council to ask if we opposed it or not. John Pearson, from Liverpool, wrote that he had no view, as there were very few pyramids to sell in Liverpool, and he thought most were in Egypt. Pyramid selling actually faded away without much public outcry, a far shout from Albania in 1996/7 where the country was reduced to anarchy as a result of Government support for pyramid selling of money. How people, however educated, could part with their life savings in mad schemes like these, as even the poor people of Albania did, defeats me. Of course the English version merely dealt in goods and chattels, not money, and I suppose the worst that could happen was that you ended up with no money, but with 2,000 Chinese dinner plates, or some such.

Brian Harris (Poole) and I spent hours creating a list of offences which carried the possibility of imprisonment, but which would never have been used in practice, and could usefully have the possibility of imprisonment removed. We uncovered some weird offences, dating back a century or more. Killing a whale was one such offence, and on enquiring the views of my colleagues, it was John Pearson again who wrote that in his time at Liverpool the villains there had committed every offence on the list, except killing a whale. Could it remain imprisonable just in case .... a Liverpudlian was bound to commit that offence sooner or later.

I mentioned the talent on the Council, and whilst it is invidious to mention names, I always was invidious. Basil and Ronald Horsman, known collectively as the cavalry, were always at the forefront of Council affairs. It was Ronald who pointed out to the then Treasurer, George Yandell, (Nottingham), in open AGM, that the printed accounts did not balance, as the expenses column was one penny out. It was, but Ronald must have been the only one to add it up. George retaliated by putting one penny on the Presidents' desk and honour was satisfied.

For sheer intellectual ability, Roger Rickard (Colchester), Brian Harris (Poole) and John Richman (Sheffield) were head and shoulders above most of us, and produced brilliant papers on topics many and varied. John eventually edited Stones' Justices' Manual for over 20 years. How the Lord Chancellor failed to appoint those three Stipendiary Magistrates, assuming they wished to be, is a mystery to this day. Especially looking back at some of the contemporary appointments, and current ones.

Pat Halnan (Cambridge) later to become a Circuit Judge, was a tower of strength, and still found time to edit Wilkinson on Road Traffic. Brian Harris (Poole) was another glutton for work, and became one of very few non-practising Q.C.s. It was said that if he didn't know something, he wrote an article about it, having been forced to research the subject. I only ever remember him being wrong once in over 10 years. It had to be. I got my copy of whatever it was he had written, and sent it to my M.P., Janet Fookes, with hardly a glance. If Brian said it, that was it. But, I got a rather tart letter back from Janet, saying the opening premise was wrong in law, proving it, and the rest was therefore pointless. Oh, woe was me, and woe was Brian. I don't think I ever dared to tell him. And so many others there were of outstanding ability, with such valuable contributions, and so little reward, except the knowledge of helping the system a little.

There were some lightweight members of the Council, only to be expected of 15 bodies, and it was obvious they were in it for an O.B.E. (later not awarded automatically to a former President, and rightly so), but they were very few. Most really did want to better conditions of their colleagues, and contribute meaningfully to the creation of new laws in the changing society.

I think I became treasurer in 1985, or thereabouts, and again methinks it was because the brains thought I could cause little damage there. I had to get the subscription up in the second year (I think it was) and had an easy ride getting the hefty rise. That surprised me. I was automatically then on the salaries committee, and the membership was upset, putting it mildly, that local government chief officers, with whom there was some salary connection, got a percentage rise one year plus £326 a year extra, whilst justices' clerks got the percentage rise, but no £326 extra. There was fighting talk. I was told a meeting had been arranged with the Labour Home Secretary, Merlyn Rees, about this £326. I was incredulous that we needed to go to the very top about a miserable £326 a year, but it was the principle I was told.

Came the day and we were ushered into the presence, and shook hands. "We" were David Kidner (Coventry), the late Bill Timpany (Kings Lynn), and me. Now I was the smallest and I am 6 feet 2 inches. Merlyn Rees appeared to be about 5 feet nothing. I was to take the lead (reluctantly I might add) and I opened by saying (spur of the moment stuff) we honestly had not chosen our biggest three, in order to intimidate him. It went down well, and there were laughs and giggles. It had never occurred to the Home Secretary that we would wish to intimidate him. That's what the man said anyway. It was his turn. "When are you going on strike then?" "Strike", I spluttered wondering what his officials had told him, "We're not going on strike, but our members are incensed that the Town Clerks of this land are spending £326 a year on gin which we cannot afford". It was not the best argument, looking back, but it created a climate. "Ah" said the Home Secretary "I see" – He visibly relaxed. "Do you mind if I smoke and would you like to?" He had his minister with him, Dr. Shirley Summerskill, violently "agin" boxing and smoking. If looks could have killed .... The three of us all smoked cigarettes, and we lit up as the Home Secretary lit his cigar, and Dr. Summerskill went pale and grimaced; well I think she did, it was difficult to see through the smoke. There was further light badinage, and the Home Secretary opined he didn't think £326 was a great problem and I said I was sure it wasn't. We left on good terms and we got the £326 within a month or two. The gin point must have swung it I always thought.

When on the Council most members who think get hi-jacked on to various multi-agency committees from time to time. I was on two or three, over the years. The first one was interesting. It was a Home Office committee to look at the very large array of maximum financial penalties and suggest something. Parliament had never had any policy on this and as each new offence was created, and there were many, some civil servant thought of a number, doubled it, and that became the maximum fine. Often it was difficult to find exactly what the maximum was, a figure tucked away in a schedule, or the last section, or nowhere. The maxima, then, ranged from five shillings, to four hundred pounds, with exceptions only for Customs and Excise offences and tax frauds where the sky was the limit. Illegal fishing in "our" waters by foreign boats later joined that exclusive band. £50,000 and forfeit the whole catch. We did it in Plymouth, fairly often. I occasionally sold the fish at Plymouth fish market. We deliberated at half a dozen meetings, and came to the conclusion in about six months that there should be five bands, A to E, with maxima for each band, £20 for A, rising gradually to E at £400. And all offences, existing and future, should be in A to E somewhere as Parliament thought fit. And there the matter remained.

I had forgotten all about it until Kenneth Cooke (Bradford, later a Stipendiary Magistrate and then a Circuit Judge), and also on the committee as a seconded justices' clerk, one day suggested I have a look at the current Criminal Justice Bill, and lo and behold our suggestions had been incorporated, virtually word for word. It had taken, as Kenneth said, just 10 years, almost to the month, for our ideas to percolate the Home Office, and get through to Ministers for a bit of action. The Home Office view at the time was that that was a bit of speedy work. Happy carefree days, begorrah.

For all the fun JCS gave to members, and friends I can only recall two bequests in wills. Lord Merthyr, a charming man, and the Chairman of the Magistrates' Association in the days before it became too pushy, left a considerable sum of money to JCS, which was converted into a beautiful goblet, and then a glass of port/brandy at the annual JCS dinner for those attending. The toast is, of course, "Lord Merthyr".

William Turner was a senior partner in the firm of solicitors Wolferstan, Snell and Turner, (now Wolferstans) in Plymouth. He was also a part-time justices' clerk for Roborough, an area just to the North of the existing city boundary, certainly before and for several years after WW2. By his will he left money to the JCS which the council decided should be used to buy a badge of office for the Vice-President. It is a splendid affair, on a green riband, and I guess Mr. Turner would have been surprised, but delighted, the justices' clerk for Plymouth was the first to wear it, as it came in my year as Vice-President.

And so it went on. Service on the council draws to a close, as one becomes vice-President, and then President.

It works on the "Buggins turn" principle, unless one has been extremely beastly to all and sundry. I had been beastly, but only to selected victims, so I suppose I just scraped in and became President in 1979, for a year. It really is a tremendous honour to lead such a superb talented group as justices' clerks, and I was not alone in wondering whether or not I was up to it all. Other former Presidents have told me it bothered them too, the enormity of it. I was lucky in having David Kidner as secretary, jolly lucky, and he kept me on the straight and narrow, so far as I could be reined in. But there is also tremendous support from the rank and file membership, although you have known most of them for ten or twenty years, so it is easy to that extent. Having thus praised justices' clerks, I must make it clear I would never have allowed my daughter to marry one.

There were then about forty geographical branches of the Society, and you were expected to get to all of them for lunch, and/or dinner if invited, and give them a chat about the goings on nationally. Roger Rickard (Colchester) was my predecessor as President and he told me always to start that chat show to members with the latest update on salary negotiations, especially if they looked good, which wasn't often. I always did what Roger told me to do, anyway, and it proved popular. I never realised until later how lucky I was, as it was in 1980, my year, that justices' clerks got the biggest pay rise ever, 30% in some cases. It was no big deal actually as we had been under-increased for the previous three –

five years, apart from the £326 special gin bonus previously mentioned, but it felt good.

I got to all branches except three, and it took some stamina. Your own office needed an occasional appearance, so the staff knew you were still alive, and you still loved them. Magistrates too liked to know you were still with them, in spirit if not in the flesh. So Sundays were used for eight or 10 hours to catch up on the paperwork. Since those days branches have amalgamated so the task now may not be quite so arduous.

Sometimes a wife would be asked to visit with the President (*his* wife I mean) and they were pleasant affairs, much enjoyed by the girls. Where to lodge the children, the dog, the rabbit and other impedimenta was another story.

Other invitations for dinner, or to speak, often both, came thick and fast: just a sample really this; the Bar, Inns of Court and Senate as it then was, Magistrates Association, Assistant Justices' Clerks' Association, Law Society, Prosecuting Solicitors' Society, Betting and Gaming Board, Registrars of County Courts, as they then were, and several others. It was my wife who summed it up beautifully when the year was over, and we were having dinner at the Lord Mayors' evening, and sat on sprig A, B, or X. She suddenly turned to me and said "Isn't it super not being on the top table." That said it all, although I know she thoroughly enjoyed her outings, every single one in that year of office. And she always got me to the right place with a spare clean shirt: not an easy task she later said.

The year ended with a conference and annual dinner at Scarborough, over which I had to preside. I was again lucky in my choice of speakers, and we all laughed heartily at Ray Dean, a Circuit Judge from Leeds whom I'd known for some years, (a bit like Al Read), Marcus Fox, the M.P., and my old friend John Pugh (Alcester, the smallest court area in the country). I must have sounded jolly dull, compared to that trio, who virtually had us rolling in the aisles.

It was years after, maybe seven or eight years, when the Plymouth Court received a Transfer of Fine Order from Bournemouth. On the bottom was written "Cliff. I still remember with nostalgia that superb Yorkshire Pudding and Onion Gravy at Scarborough." That is as good a way as any to end a chapter.

Except to say that a few years later, on retirement, I was offered Honorary Membership of JCS, the highest honour the Society can bestow. The Society has some thirty Honorary Members, mostly former Presidents and former holders of high judicial office, like Lord Denning. The awards are often made by the President in "public" at JCS functions. I made the award to Lord Elwyn-Jones at a Council dinner at the Law Society and the recipients offer thanks after receiving a Scroll, setting out some of their achievements. Thanks are given in a variety of ways, charming, witty, nostalgic, but the best I ever heard was from John Martin (Lowestoft) before a full conference dinner. He composed it walking on the beach in East

Anglia, and it was never committed to writing, until it
had been delivered, when some of us insisted on the
written word, as we knew it would go down to posterity.
This is it.

"Good president, good members, honoured guests;
Seems it to me that I must first explain
The manner of my speech; 'tis thus, that when
The tidings first came to my ken that there
Should come to pass what you have seen this night,
And hot-foot on those tidings trod the thought
That I must needs give thanks, then on that
thought
I pondered long, and mused – how best
discharge
With fitting elegance so grave a task?
And, as I mused, there came to me a Muse,
Fair daughter of great Zeus, Euterpe called,
And one of sisters nine. When we had kissed
(For we had met before), said she: "Good John,
It is not meet to give such thanks as those
That you do need to give in common prose –
However well bespiced with lewd joke
Or with Hartwellian quip or anecdote.
Would Chaucer, Spenser, Milton (!),
Wordsworth, Pope
Or even A.P.H. have sunk so low?
No, no: it must take nobler shape, and if
Your thoughts should turn to verse, I say
beware
Of rhymed couplet, that so easy may

To jingling doggerel fall; there is one style
of speech that suits the hour, and that the verse
Well called 'heroic' favoured by great Will.
In iambic pentametric lines
You shall declaim!" – and saying so, was gone,
And here I stand, and you that list do hear
Me speak as Hamlet spake, or Ferdinand -
Of Caliban, belike you'll shake your heads
And say 'ere I be done – with here and there,
As suits the mode, some spondee foot, perhaps.
Or anapaest – "Who pissed?" I hear? For
shame!
Cliff Moiser's voice, I swear. Pay him no heed,
Nor say "Two short, one long", he'll
comprehend
You ill, and vow you gave an order at
The bar. But I digress 'ere I begin;
They say 'twas ever such with men of law.
Do you remember dear old Stanley Green
(God rest his soul)? He never could abide
The point. Where was I, Sir? – Ah, I recall;
The point. Well said. Now must I to my task.
For ten short lines I would put off that which
I pass for wit; 'tis feeble stuff and but
A cloak to hide that I am moved, and say
That I do rate this honour you bestow
Not less than touch of Sovereign's blade.
Should I be dubbed, I would as lief that I should hear
Men say, whereas that they might say: "There goes
A knight – call him 'Sir John'", that they

should say:
"There stands an honorary member of
The J.C.S." (Fewer they be than knights.)
'tis scarce enough that I should say my say;
'twere fitter had I brought to Windermere
A dozen rows of strings, some trumpets and
A flute or two – with Previn on the stick! -
And sung a canzonetta in B flat
(A grateful key – 'twas Schubert called it so -
And by that token fit for gratitude).
Instead there's nothing more to say
Except to indicate the end of act
Or scene as would the Bard I dare to ape.
And so, I take my scroll from Windermere
To set it on a wall (choosing a spot
not so deep hid that others may not read
Its words as well as I) until maybe,
When dotage comes, I'll half believe them
true.
I go. Farewell, God bless you all. Adieu."

Chapter 6

People

Justices' clerks meet many Very Important People, in the course of the job, mostly on social occasions, and occasionally in the dock. Being a member of the Council of the Justices' Clerk's Society increased the socialising with VIPs considerably.

Lord Denning must be at the top of any judges' list. He was a great supporter of justices' clerks and I suspect one unknown justices' clerk, a hero somewhere, had been kind to him when he was a young barrister appearing in some obscure magistrates' court for the first time. Lord Denning attended every justices' clerks' dinner when he could, and he opened many a new magistrates court house; given the chance I suspect that he would have opened them all. He opened the "new" magistrates court in Plymouth (taken over by the Crown Court in 1971) in 1963, or thereabouts. But he had an affinity with Plymouth, that was little known. In fact he was appointed (old style) Recorder of Plymouth during World War II, about 1942, but never sat as such as he was elevated to the High Court Bench before he could get there. But he loved the City.

Nancy Astor was the first woman Member of Parliament and she represented one of the Plymouth divisions. Before she died she gave her home, a beautiful house on Elliot Terrace, overlooking the Hoe, to the City for such use as the Lord Mayor saw fit. The contents of the house were included in the gift, and there is a super picture of the Queen Mother, as Queen, with the inscription "Do you remember the first bananas coming into Plymouth after years without". It was dated 1943. There was also a superb loo, now gone alas, but I saw it – fully four feet across on a one foot high plinth. Winston Churchill regarded this highly, and named it "The Throne". You could write a book on Nancy Astor alone. A Flag Officer, Plymouth (never less than Rear-Admiral) was to take Lady Astor out to dinner one night, and arranged for a Royal Navy car to take them both to a suitable Navy Mess. Lady Astor asked the Admiral if he minded calling at a house in Devonport, just for a few minutes as she needed to see a constituent about a pressing matter. No problem, except when they arrived the constituent, a lady, was out. The door was opened by the daughter of the house, about ten years of age. She said her mother was out, but surveying the scene, she said, "But you can come in. My mother said that if any lady came with a sailor, I was to let her have the front room, but only for half an hour and it costs ten shillings." The story never included what the Admiral said.

But I digress. The Astor house, as it is known, lay heavy on the hands of the Lord Mayor who really didn't know what to do with it. Repairs had to be done, the place decorated and staff kept there for very occasional use indeed. I knew this and got the then Lord Mayor, a friend, to allow Lord and Lady Denning to stay there for a few days at a time, I suppose they came down five or six times in the Seventies and early Eighties. Joan Denning could paint a little, but often sat simply admiring the magnificent view out to sea. They both joined in a little socialising, but the point of the visit was to get away from it all, and relax. I took them across the Tamar, to Mount Edgecumbe for viewing the stately home and tea with the Earl, or rather Tony Bowden, a local magistrate, did in his speedboat. Very exhilarating. We also had many pleasant outings on Dartmoor. One visit coincided with the annual conference of the National Association of Justices' Clerks' Assistants, as it then was, in Plymouth. Whilst there were to be no formal engagements, Lord and Lady Denning both got to their dinner, after some gentle persuasion by me, and he made an after-dinner speech which brought the house down. The assistants, who gave him a spontaneous standing ovation, were delighted because they didn't even know he was in Plymouth and he was their late unknown "extra". Some extra.

The judgement of the European Court in Luxembourg concerning the *Christine Marie*, the fishing case (see Cases) came as one of his books, *The Closing Chapter*, was at the proof stage, and he was in Plymouth: he got the proofs back, so he could add a few paragraphs about it. The judgement was really what he had preached for years, that if there was a gap in the law, the courts could fill it. This point of view was not generally accepted at the time, but yet again, Lord Denning was ahead of the field.

When Lord Denning retired, the Justices' Clerk's Society presented him with a shepherd's crook, a beautiful crafted affair with silver bands. John Jenkins (Tredegar) knew the craftsmen to make it. It was typical of Lord Denning that he telephoned me a year or two later, to indicate that on his death he wanted it returned to the Society, and we discussed ways to do that.

That Astor house was eventually put to good use from 1972 when Plymouth became for the first time a Crown Court Centre, with visiting High Court judges staying there. Before that, the High Court judges were at Bodmin or Exeter only. There were hiccups at first and one judge (or his wife) became a bit rattled about the antics of the cook, who with the butler, was hired by the City on a casual basis for the two week visit. The butler was alright, hired from the Holiday Inn, but the cook, Oh dear. The judge (or his wife) was right; enquiries by the police ascertained he was hired from a shipping company, straight off a merchant ship docking in Plymouth. He had 17 previous convictions, and was known to be mentally unstable. He had to go. I got there as a guest for dinner one night just before he departed hence, and I swear the Avocado Pear could only have been tackled with a hammer (large) and chisel. But things became better with a permanent butler and housekeeper.

Lord Chief Justices often addressed justices' clerks at dinners or training seminars, and I was fortunate, if that is the right word, to see and hear Lord Goddard, old "Blood and Guts" as he was called. I well remember him giving a talk in Worcester in the early Sixties when he must have been approaching 80 years of age, and he gave a good argument then for bringing back the stocks for miscreants. Humiliation was the point. Alas nothing came of it. When he died Bernard Levin, a nasty little journalist, wrote a really scathing obituary in the *Times*: I indicated to the *Times*, as did many other people, that it was way over the top, quite unfair, and should never have been published. I said I would never buy the *Times* again, and I have not done so.

I had a very short spell at Wokingham in Berkshire where the justices' clerk was, well, a bit short sighted and tended to rush in ...... The Bench Chairman asked his opinion about some legal point, and he avowed it had been quite simple until a recent case, obviously wrongly decided by Lord Goddard, quite unnecessarily and not favourably. The Chairman allowed him to go on for about five minutes, and when he paused for breath, she said "Oh, really. How interesting I'm Lord Goddard's sister". She was too.

Lord Widgery was not unpopular, but he worked on towards the end when he was ill and should have retired. He blotted his copy book in that period at a justices' clerks' conference attended by over 250 people by opening thus: "I have not had time to write anything for you and I propose to read the paper I gave to the Canadian Bar Association last month". Some of us felt like walking out, but did not as we were hosts and courtesy does matter. The affair was put right by John Jenkins (Tredegar) later that day at dinner, when proposing a toast to the guests, unfortunately, I thought after Lord Widgery had gone home. "I am sorry", he said, "I have not had time to write anything for you and I propose to use the speech I prepared for the Bedwelty Rotary club last month". Happy days.

Of the top civil servants we met, the most competent, caring and charming was Sir Thomas Skyrme K.C.V.O., C.B., C.B.E., T.D., J.P., D.L., M.A., the secretary of Commissions in the Lord Chancellor's office, I suppose the equivalent of a permanent secretary. In my view he was a great friend of all justices' clerks, not just the few. I spent most of my working life trying to avoid the Honours List (and joining Rotary), but Tom seems to have attracted Honours like flies to a jam-pot, although I believe he did avoid Rotary. Rumour has it that after a distinguished WW2 career, he went to the Lord Chancellor's office as a temporary job in 1947 – and then remained there until he retired in the Eighties. The department consisted of Tom, two boys and four ladies in 1947, it is said, but now employs hundreds. I think it was more efficient in 1947 than now. Tom always found time to listen and talk about problems you might have in any sphere, but especially with magistrates, mostly delicate, and I cannot think of any occasion when I would not have done exactly what he suggested. He was sound in every way and simply oozed common sense. The system was the worse for his retirement.

Possibly the less said the better about civil servants in other government agencies. The Home Office certainly had some high flyers, often with a first at Oxbridge, but the system beat them. It was at York in 1972 at a justices' clerks' conference that I first knew of real problems. There were two Home Office officials visiting us and they were quite high in the hierarchy, only two or three points below a permanent secretary, whatever that is called. The problem for them was which train to catch back to London, the 11.30 or the 12.30. They could neither agree nor decide, and in the end the justices' clerks' President actually made the decision for them, and wisely chose the 11.30 as he'd had enough.

These Home Office officials were mostly very serious, but just occasionally you could see a glimmer. I was at one meeting in the Home Office and the senior civil servant asked if we minded their latest entry sitting in. Of course not. In she came, definitely a first at Oxbridge, because she had on a rugby shirt in startling colours and jeans which blended well with our dark business suits. We lit our cigarettes, and one innocent noted aloud that no Home Office official smoked "No" said the stripling, "They're mostly on Cannabis". She *was* joking – I think.

I sent a letter of congratulations and best wishes to one Home Office lady who retired at 60, after being Head of a Department for several years. I saw fit (generous that I was) to say I was sorry I'd written her some stinking letters over the years, over perceived Home Office errors. She wrote back and said I need not apologise, she personally always looked forward to hearing from me as my letters, thought by some to be occasionally vituperous, brightened many a dull Home Office day. She quite made my day, which was not the point of the correspondence at all.

The late Lord Elwyn Jones followed Gerald Gardiner as Labour Lord Chancellor, again a good friend of justices' clerks. He was a good Lord Chancellor responsible for updating the magisterial system when he could. He achieved fame as a thorough prosecutor at the Nuremburg trials after WW2, but he started out modestly. In August 1939 he was a corporal, in the anti-aircraft T.A., and sent to Plymouth with, I think, five bombardiers, with orders to defend the City from the German Luftwaffe. They had one Lewis gun, and a few rounds of ammunition, but took up station on top of Aggie Westons (sailors rest), living in time off at Bull Point barracks not too far away. Disaster struck when within a month, one of the bombardiers was summoned to appear at Torpoint magistrates' court, to face a charge of stealing a set of dominoes from a Torpoint pub. It looked bad as the dominoes were found in the bombardiers kitbag on a search. Elwyn telephoned his C.O. in London, who happened to be a solicitor, and asked what to do. "You're a barrister" (just) said the C.O., "You can take instructions from me to defend him, do your best". He did.

At the hearing some days later the first problem was to get into the courtroom, the door of which was guarded by a twenty stone policeman. "Can you tell me what time X's case might be on?" asked Elwyn. Reply, cynically, "You X then?" "No, I'm his barrister." "Garn", said the policeman who had not seen many barristers in a corporals' uniform in Torpoint magistrates' court. But he got in after further discussion. In 1975 he could still remember the case in detail. The licensee of the pub gave evidence, and yes, those dominoes belonged to the pub, and the accused had been in there several nights drinking in the last month: he had no right to take any dominoes. The questions in cross-examination by Elwyn were few.

"Did the accused play dominoes in the pub?" "Yes". "Every night when he was in the pub?". "Yes". "Did you ask him, indicating he was a good player, if he would play in your pub team?" "Yes, I did" "Did he say he would?" "Yes, if he could get away" "If he had said to you, 'If I am going to play for the pub team I shall need to borrow some dominoes to practice with, there's none at Bull Point" what would you have said?" "I should have told him to take them with pleasure". Equals collapse of case. I tried to get a copy of the court record at Torpoint court, so he could use it in his book *In My Time* but the records for 1939 were gone, destroyed in the blitz, alas. It always amused him that he had risen to the highest judicial office in the land, but in the valleys he was only referred to as "Idris' brother", Idris achieving much more fame by playing rugby for Wales. As we agreed, the Welsh usually got their priorities right.

Barry Rose has long been my friend and a friend to all justices' clerks. He is the proprietor (I think that is the right word) I believe since 1947, of the *Justice of the Peace and Local Government Law*. The name of the journal had varied fractionally over the years but the words "Justice of the Peace" have long been there. It is reputedly the oldest law report in the U.K., appears weekly without fail, and is known by all as the J.P. Barry also owns Barry

Rose (Publishers) Ltd., and publishes *Family Law* among other legal journals.

I think I first wrote for the J.P. in 1960, or thereabouts and I much welcomed the cheque for three guineas which was spent on drink, as I recall. I have written for all the legal journals (except the *Criminal Law Review*) over the years, but the greatest pleasure always comes from being published in the JP. The fees were modest, but contributed greatly, I worked out, to the school fees for my daughter, Penelope Jane. If the written word didn't pay well the lecture fees did . We ran several training courses for magistrates but they ended after a couple of years. I tended to use four or five star hotels, like the Holiday Inn in Plymouth, but an official from the Lord Chancellor's office said outright these were too opulent for magistrates. I said that perhaps magistrates should attend university or similar accommodation and sleep in student beds, at 2 feet 6 inches wide, and eat from plastic top tables. He said yes. The funny point was that I was fairly friendly with Holiday Inns, and their top executives, (Tom Skyrme once alleged I had shares in Holiday Inns) and had negotiated accommodation terms, roughly the same as two feet six inches wide beds, with plastic table top eating in academe. We carried on with lawyers training courses though, for some years when I acted as Course Director, and with modest success, and only the odd failure.

Barry was ever one for innovation, and he produced several training audio tapes. I made the first tape on Bail. The trouble was that with Barry you had to have lunch, or dinner. Simpsons on the Strand, the Oxford and Cambridge Club, or similar. He booked the studio in North London for the recording of the bail tape at say 4.00pm., and said we'd have lunch. As it was the first one, he wanted to hear me record. It was a good lunch, his lunches always were, and as we arrived at the studio, the chap in charge asked who was making the tape. We said I was. "Um", he said, "Well drink all that black coffee there, while I set up the recording machine". I thought it was a bit uncalled for, and the only difficulty I had was pronouncing "impracticability", well anyone would. I should just have used different words, to the same effect. Words of one syllable preferably.

Two of the better items in the J.P. were Notes of the Week and Brougham (of law and lawyers) and I graduated under Brian Harris, as Editor, to writing sometimes for those two and the anonymity I thought I would achieve. My eldest son read the J.P. in the library, and with unerring accuracy indicated the bits I wrote, and the bits I didn't. But I doubt anyone else could tell. Barry still wears a bowler hat in town, and enjoys his London (club) jaunts from Bognor Regis. He will be missed by justices' clerks when (if) he retires and I cannot see the likes of him coming again. More's the pity.

Of colleagues there were so many good guys and just a few not so good. One of the good ones (mostly misunderstood by the County) was Niall Campbell, the erstwhile justices' clerk at Barnstaple. There were but four justices' clerks who had been Royal Marines during WW2, Spiller from Eastbourne I think it was, the late

George Wilkinson who I succeeded at Dudley when he was appointed at the seat of learning Cambridge, Niall and me. I think Niall is a few days older than me, but I joined the Royal Marines a few weeks before him so I am the senior. He told some delightful tales of 1943. We both joined as ordinary marines, and did the basic training which was pretty arduous, though we survived. Now Niall really is a descendant of the Campbells who were coming, hurrah, hurrah, and has some blue blood – he became the 8th baronet when his father died hence Sir Niall. Alas, he inherited Barcadine castle up yonder near Oban, but no money which was a bit disastrous although by 1997 it is a thriving tourist attraction through much family hard work. But to 1943. He was a qualified marine, and then told his Lance-Corporal he thought he should be commissioned. He got a very short negative answer, two words in fact. Similar ones, maybe less colourful, from the Corporal, the Sergeant, the Colour Sergeant, the Sergeant-Major, the 2nd Lieutenant, the Lieutenant, and the company commander. However, he persisted, and the colonel (knowing of the blue blood?) thought it a jolly good idea and off Niall went to the O.C.T.U. He passed out, he always wondered how, and was a probationary acting temporary second lieutenant, sent with eight other second lieutenants to Stonehouse barracks here in Plymouth on a Saturday. The Regimental Sergeant-Major (it must have been Ashby who I knew well) looked them up and down – I can picture his face even now and the look of disbelief on it – and posed the question "Who has the loudest voice here?" The other eight turned and pointed to Niall, as one man. "Right" said the RSM, "You are in charge of church parade, 10.00 hours tomorrow morning" and off he went. Came the dawn, and at 09.45 there were 400 Royal Marines of various shapes and sizes, standing to attention on the parade ground. Niall took his place at the front and a sergeant came up, saluted smartly and said "Church parade ready to move off, Sir". Niall said "Carry on Sergeant," being the only words he remembered from officers school. But the Sergeant, luckily, was equal to it, and indicated that Niall should turn round, shout "Parade to Church, Quick March" and set off. He did just that, but unfortunately, as he passed under the main arch into Durnford Street, he realised he did not know where the church was. No one but Niall could set off not knowing. In fact, if you turn left the church is on the left, some 300 yards away. His version is that he tossed the imaginary proverbial coin, which indicated go right, which he did. The sergeant, in a dilemma, took 400 troops left, and Niall describes graphically how it feels to lead 400 men, with their feet thudding the road going away from you in the opposite direction. I know the "pit of the stomach" comes into it. But he got himself out of that quite unexpectedly. Realising what had happened, he turned first left, and left again, leading no one, and came to the parallel street with Durnford Street, Cremyl Street. The Sergeant, also realising what had happened and being also quick witted, led the troops first right, and right again, and they all joined up in Cremyl Street and went merrily the right way to church, there to sing lustily, or at least Niall did, "Oh God, Our Help in Ages Past"

I was always big myself on church parades and services and when the justices' clerks met in weekend training conferences, often at Jesus College, there was always a Church Service to attend on the Sunday. It surprised me at first to hear how loudly justices' clerks sang hymns, and it took me a year or two to work out the words in the hymn, "Father of Mankind". They should have sung "Forgive our foolish ways", but one very senior justices' clerk, refusing to accept he had any, always sang, "Forgive their foolish ways", at the same time glaring at several of his colleagues who he thought were not quite up to the job. He was a Christian, too.

I think I worked it out in my first year as a justices' clerk that I was nothing if my staff were inadequate or not up to it, and I have been blessed with quite superb deputies and staff, hardly a duff one amongst them. I was very lucky. It is quite amazing to me how talented the staff became if given the chance and encouragement – not just good at the job, but in achieving academic success. I encouraged when I could. At the last count, and in my time, or just after, we turned out from the Plymouth, in-house staff:

1 barrister

3 solicitors

7 diplomas in magisterial law

3 Law degrees (LLB)

3 (Post Grad) diplomas in management studies

Not bad considering the entire clerical staff only numbered a little over 40, and most of the academic successes were by youngsters who had left school at 16, with four or five 'O' levels, if that. I was truly proud of them all. We even had a court caretaker reading for an 'O' level in law, which gives an idea of what can be achieved with a bit of encouragement. I am grateful to every one of them for making my job easier.

I was also blessed, over 30 years, with quite superb Bench Chairmen. The various magistrates I served unerringly went for high quality, in the likes of Leonard Hillman and Luing Preedy at Dudley, and Geoffrey Leatherby, Isobel Adam, Charles Evans, Jim Woodrow and Judy Veale at Plymouth. How they struck gold every time I will never know. It was not always so in many other areas.

Lord Foot (John, the brother of Michael Foot) was a Plymouth solicitor, and had virtually retired when I got there. They said that when he prosecuted for the police, he did more for the defence than any defending lawyer ever did. He was a charming man of quite liberal views, as befits the Foot family. I must admit I was quite surprised when he showed interest in one of my wants. I had been bothered by the maximum eight clear days for any remand in custody, as prosecutions slowed down, and there was this weekly trail of prisoners under escort from jail to court, and back after a two minute appearance. A costly job and each prisoner had three or four appearances. In our case it was 45 miles each way using Exeter prison. Cornwall had dreadful distances.

John asked me to see him and give reasons for increasing the limit to 21 days, and I did. He took down the reasons on the back of an envelope, and said he agreed. There was a current Criminal Justice Bill before the Lords, at Committee stage, and he put down an amendment I drafted, which merely decreed "delete 8 and insert 21" in the appropriate section of the existing law. I still have the copy of Hansard where the argument was put by John Foot in the most beautiful English, and I guess from the back of the envelope. He was a persuasive advocate, and the government Minister (trying to save money no doubt) said he agreed in principle, and if Lord Foot would withdraw the amendment, the government would draft it to the same effect, but with a couple of safeguards in there. He did. The Home Office knew I was behind it, and 'ere long, I received a draft of their proposals. It took two or three pages of close typed new sections to replace my "delete 8 and insert 21".

Meanwhile, back at t'mill, opposition from the do-gooders emerged, led by Joe Brayshaw, my friend, and then Secretary to the Magistrates' Association. They alleged that 21 days would become the norm, not eight days and this was dreadful for liberty. They overlooked the fact that no trial, or committal for trial, took place in *under* 21 days then, but they won the day, and the amendment was lost at Third Reading (or Report Stage). It goes without saying (I aver) that the law was changed to exactly what we proposed seven or eight years later, when the Home Office worked out the cost of transporting prisoners, with escorts, on the weekly unnecessary jaunt to court. In the meantime, the times between arrest and trial or committal for trial had increased considerably and the 21 days should probably have been 28 or 30 days, maybe even more with the advent of the Crown Prosecution Service.

For 30 years and more I enjoyed my relationship with the media, which is certainly not the view of many, probably most, justices' clerks.

Nationally, I knew Marcel Berlins, legal correspondent of the *Times*, and Terry Shaw, acting similarly for the *Telegraph*. They are terrific journalists in Division 1. So knowledgeable. Down to local court reporting level, Joe Brookes for the *Wolverhampton Express and Star*, Norman Shaw of the *Birmingham Post and Mail*, and Jill Slight of the *Western Evening Herald* were all first rate reporters, and I considered them friends. Courts make queer decisions from time to time, and I encouraged local reporters to telephone and ask if there was something odd or unusual; there was often a reason even if it could not be made public. I never had a single confidence broken in an off-the-record comment. I mention television, which I thoroughly enjoyed, elsewhere.

Chapter 7

Foreign Parts

In *Dewsbury Boy*, I wrote of seeing Russian Cossacks at the Dewsbury Rugby Football ground in the late Thirties, the finest display of horsemanship I have ever seen. If anyone had then told me that within five years I would be in Murmansk, or the Kola inlet, as gun crew on a Royal Navy escort ship for war-time convoys, with tanks and aeroplanes for Russia, I would have said they were silly. If anyone had then told me that within 50 years, I would be travelling regularly to Moscow and St. Petersburg, to meet and talk shop (not forgetting to socialise heavily) with some of the finest lawyers and judges in Russia, I would have said they were mad. But so it was, and I still have so many good friends in those two cities.

Mind you, I didn't start off so well with Russians. It was October 1943, and after a rough convoy passage my ship reached the Kola Inlet, in North Russia, and I managed a few hours ashore in those frozen wastes near Murmansk. I tried to get back some land legs you know. The first person I saw after leaving the docks was a Russian soldier guarding the dock gates or a nearby building – and the soldier was a young woman, most attractive, but with a rifle slung across her shoulder. Ever

one to foster good relations with our allies, especially
female, I started to chat her up, gently, which wasn't easy,
she speaking only Russian, me speaking only English. I
knew there was a wooden shack up the hill (past the
public gallows!) where I could get a sit down and a cup
of, well what? I was told coffee but it turned out to be
vodka in fact. Now all I wanted to do, to start with
anyway, was take the girl out for a cup of coffee when
she came off duty. I smiled a lot, well you do at 18 years
old, and gesticulated wildly about the coffee house, but
it was there where I went wrong I think. She smiled, but
she also unslung her rifle, and with the safety catch off I
noticed, prodded me with the gun, gently it is true, up
the hill towards the shack – alone. It was the first time
my Royal Marine uniform had let me down with the
other sex and I can only think that it was because, *a)*
communication had not been good with our female Allies
about Royal Marines, OR *b)* if it had, my large sheepskin
coat covered my uniform. When I came back to my ship
the attractive girl guard had gone, replaced by a feller –
Ugh. I slunk past. But it all got better and I shrugged off
this poor start.

I had been to America a few times, giving the odd
lecture or two, and somehow got the urge to get further
afield to a different culture, even though the Americans
were so friendly, generous and hospitable. I intimated
my wish to visit Russia to the Home Office in the early
Seventies, and got the then "usual" reply. The Foreign
Office had indicated that the Russians were a set of
bounders, and I would do well to keep clear. I left it there

but as I could see the political climate change, I went back to it a year or two later, and to my surprise the Home Office told me the Foreign Office thought the time might well be ripe for an exchange of legal visits, and views. I was given the name and address of the Secretary of the Moscow Bar Association, Helen Alferova, and virtually by return of post she indicated how welcome we would be. She was not wrong. The team paid its own expenses, some £400 each, but I got £100 each, back from the British Council, which I thought was generous. It turned out a superb team, most of whom didn't know each other beforehand, and to this day we meet at least annually, for dinner and even jaunts to other foreign climes, including San Sebastian and Cork.

The team was led by me, (you have to have a leader in Russia), although the deputy leader attempted a coup by leaving me stranded outside the Kremlin walls one day. Luckily I got a taxi back to the hotel, and was in time for lunch and the afternoon seminar. The attempt failed. The deputy leader was Eric Crowther, then a London Stipendiary Magistrate, with John Richman, the justices' clerk at Sheffield, Dr. (now Professor) John Baldwin of Birmingham University, Cliff Gammon, the senior partner of William Wright and Co., Solicitors, Dudley (my first pupil) and David Tonner, a computer executive at Unysis making up the team.

In many ways the Russian system of courts is like our own, except there are no juries. Most cases, criminal and civil, are decided by a judge and two assessors, but when you get to really serious criminal cases, murder, rape and the like, (our Crown Court) there are three judges who decide guilt or innocence, and sentence where appropriate. The country was divided into court areas, similar to circuits or magistrate court divisions here, and it all worked rather well, certainly in the late Eighties. Democracy brought problems, and certainly more crime, no doubt about it. The assessors, a bit like magistrates, were taken from the factory or workplace, engineers, teachers, nurses and the like and had to sit two or three weeks a year, the employer, often the state, having to pay them whilst they served. We met several assessors and it was clear they did not always agree with the judge and he or she could be outvoted on guilt or sentence. One of the highlights of that first visit was a call at the All-Union Institute for Justice Workers in Moscow. The head was the ebullient Lev Khaldeev, a delightful man with a very talented staff. We thought it was a meeting with a few members of his staff, but we were ushered into a large conference room, to the platform, with a standing ovation from over 60 judges from all over Russia (as it then was). They knew who we were, but we only found out who they were after the seminar started. Communications is not a Russian strong point. Luckily I had briefed our team each to talk for ten minutes on a subject, which taken with the others, gave a brief but wide overview of our system of justice. This went down well, but not so well as the question and answer session afterwards, lasting well over another hour. Nothing is much different worldwide, and there were problems and complaints about poor pay for the judges, bad working conditions in pretty ropey court accommodation, lack of equipment, even typewriters, so that much work was handwritten. Maybe the biggest surprise was that the state prosecutor decided whether an accused was in custody, or on the equivalent of bail. None of the judges had visited a prison, as it was not their concern. They simply accepted that as it was, but expressed much interest in jury trials, and several, a few, were in favour of giving jury trials a go, even if only as pilot schemes. I think two of us advised caution at introducing jury trials, which we said were far from perfect, especially in complex fraud cases. We were applauded by the many for saying that. We then adjourned to the professor's room, for wine, soft drinks, or tea, and a selection of cakes to make anyone's mouth water. Usual Russian hospitality, and those meringues, gosh they were superb. I went back to the institute in later years, and was delighted to see our photographs, very large, on display in the visitor V.I.P. room, many taken as we were propounding some point from the platform. Retraining of all judges in Russia is compulsory, not less often than every five years, and for four to six weeks residential tuition.

We sat in on trials in courts, not half so well equipped as the Institute, and heard cases of dangerous driving, rape and similar. Even a guilty plea is examined by the court, and in criminal cases the proof required is "beyond reasonable doubt".

The social side was not forgotten, and it was in Moscow, after three nights at the Bolshoi, that I tentatively enquired of our interpreter where the boxing or rugby was taking place. I was put in touch with the President and Chairman of the Moscow Slava rugby club, and they sent a car to the hotel to take me to their ground and see a game, which, as chance had it, was a trial for the Russian team to visit England. A Slava player was captain of that touring side eventually. After the game we adjourned to the Slava clubhouse, and talked late into the night over an enormous buffet, and wine (from Georgia), whisky (Bells), Vodka (the real stuff), brandy (Napoleon) and beer. My chauffeur drank not at all. As a result, I took two teams to Moscow, and Slava made two visits here to the South-West. The rugby they played was good quality and great fun, but the admin. for it all, mostly on my shoulders, was exhausting; albeit very worthwhile.

The Moscow Slava rugby club is sponsored by number 2 watch company, sometime Sekonda watches. The Russians are spontaneously generous, to an extreme, and load you with presents, small and large. My home is full of clocks, a teapot, a wooden horse, a plate (I love Moscow), an alarm clock and several wristlet watches. When I visit Moscow now I am under wifely instructions – No more clocks.

But the rugby management has friends in High Places, and with one of my teams we visited the Space Control Centre, just outside Moscow, Mission Control for Mir now. We actually heard space control talking to their cosmonaut "up there" and we followed its flight through space (then over Indonesia) on a massive wall chart. We met several quite famous cosmonauts, including Vladimir Lyachov who had spent 333 days in space. He drove up to the centre in a battered old Lada. A delightful man. Lunch at the Centre was impressive, with more watch presentations. We were the first "foreigners" apart from government science specialists to visit. The Watch Company owns a river boat (sleeps 40) and we enjoyed a day down river, much beer and vodka, and lunch aboard or a BBQ.

We dined at the home of Mikhail Rosenberg, a lawyer, one glorious night, where his mother did the cooking. Mikhail's father and grandfather had both been lawyers in Moscow, so he was carrying on the family tradition. What a meal, and it got a bit boisterous, well it would with the alcohol being put about. There is this custom about giving toasts in vodka, starting early in the meal, and we toasted each other, our respective countries, friendship, Mr. Gorbachev, Mrs. Thatcher and so on. I well recall the 17th toast, by me, my fourth, which was "Yorkshire County Cricket Club". I do not think our Russian hosts quite followed that one, but everyone drank to the club and the cricket should have prospered with such a lavish toast. The way to drink Vodka for the uninitiated, is to gulp it straight down in one, but take maybe a piece of bread at the same time. I became quite good at it. We sang, Old English songs, even Russian folk songs, and after a rather noisy version of Rule Britannia, I asked Mikhail how the neighbours might take all this, at 1am in the morning. He answered to the effect, no problem, they'd all be round to join in if invited.

Details of this visit, and other Russian interchanges can be found in the *Justice of the Peace (Journal)* for 5th August 1989, 12th August 1989, and 22nd June 1991, if anyone is further interested.

Over the years I spent more time in St. Petersburg than Moscow in fact, and I found that City, Leningrad, when I first went, quite delightful, although I am told the last couple of years have been horrendous, crime multiplying at an absurd rate. Tamara Khazharskaya was the secretary of the local bar, and she got many doors to open for us. Her friend Ireena was the deputy Minister of Justice, later to become senior Circuit Judge of St. Petersburg, which she still is. The police chief, Arcadi Kramerov, made us welcome, and set before us, after a visit to the cells at various police stations, possibly the most sumptuous lunch I have ever seen. We did not do it justice, as we had another meeting at 5pm alas. The table positively groaned under the weight of the caviar, sturgeon, yes, sturgeon, other fish, lamb, pork, and superb salad galore. The sweets, there must have been a dozen or so, were out of this world. There was wine, champagne and vodka and the beer looked on un-touched. In the course of animated conversations we found that in any street fracas, or public violent disorder, the chief had ordered that policewomen be immediately withdrawn, and when I expressed my total agreement, the charming lady police inspector with us said "But we women have other weapons" and gave me a knowing wink. Two of us were presented with quite beautiful watches, Leningrad etched on the back, and occasionally given to civilians who had assisted the police, as a reward.

I found the war cemetery at St. Petersburg most moving, on a par, only more so, with Arlington cemetery across the Potomac in Washington, U.S.A. It is often forgotten that Leningrad was under siege for some three years in WW2, and more people died from starvation and the cold than from German bombs and shells. At the entrance to the cemetery is a small museum with memorabilia from those dreadful days. In one glass case is a piece of bread, maybe two inches by two inches, if that, and that was the ration of bread per person per day. As visitors move slowly round the mass graves, beautifully kept, quiet music is switched on the tannoy, and one day I was approached by a member of the cemetery staff who asked me, in perfect English, what I thought of the music, did it reflect the right mood? I think it was Borodin. Well, it was sombre, as it should be, but I thought Beethoven's 5th could be used. Lo and behold, the next time I was there out over the tannoy came Beethoven's 5th, played in a very subdued way and so quietly. Across the road from the entrance is a flower shop, which will not take dollars, only roubles, and I always buy some red roses to place on one particular mass grave. Very moving, but so very rewarding remembering.

I have been several times to the Kirov, and twice I struck gold, with Swan Lake. I used to sit at the Kirov, and the Bolshoi in Moscow as well, thinking how lucky I was just being there, when so many people I know just wanted the chance to be there watching and listening. Especially when Eric Crowther intimated I was a philistine! That was simply because my favourite choice of opera was Carmen, full of violence, jealousy, rage and sex, which I think he is "agin". I have now stopped going to the Hermitage, on the basis I shall be offered a room there by the staff, so often did I go.

In 1979 the Magistrates Association got an invitation to visit the European Court in Luxembourg, and very kindly included David Kidner (Coventry), and me in the group of a dozen or so. It was very revealing and I think was the start, or confirmation anyway, of my anti-European Union views. The sheer luxury of the court building was breathtaking, plush armchairs in the courtrooms with built in five language instantaneous translation into the headphones at the touch of a button. We ate in the restaurant, equivalent certainly to a four star hotel dining room, and there appeared no difficulty over the liquor licence, assuming they bothered to get one. We were actually given pocket money for incidentals during our few days stay. Then at least half of the cases were concerned only with the court staff disputes with each other, over salary, expenses, promotion, time off with pay, and so on. There appeared to be a need for more work from member countries, and we were encouraged to create some of it, quite shamelessly I thought. No doubt the same encouragement was given to legal/judge groups visiting from other member states, and the "real" work did increase over the next few years, often to the discomfort of the Establishment of those member states.

This last ten years has seen public allegations of unfairness, and political decisions by the European Court. There would appear to be some truth in some of the allegations, and I must say I can see no justification for that court being able to over-rule our courts, certainly on our internal matters. But then, I am a Euro-sceptic of Division I. David and I bought European Court ties but I suspect he never wears his, and I never wear mine.

America The land of the free. When I was 40 I made a list of some ten events I wished to undergo before I expired. Some cost nothing, some a few pounds only, and some fairly expensive, like visiting America – in fact it cost me nothing, or very little as the cards fell.

Incidentally, one of the cheap or nil cost desires was to attend a Foyles literary luncheon, which I did (courtesy of Barry Rose), at the Grosvenor Hotel in London. I met the fabulous, to me, Christina Foyle who presided, and indeed I was seated at the top table near her. The book launch was Philip Larkin's *Book of English Prose*, and I found his conversation quite stimulating. The whole thing was a brilliant affair and I must return another day. I gave up my taxi at the conclusion of luncheon to a most attractive female film star, but it got me nowhere, alas, except to make me feel good and chivalrous.

But back to America, I made a few enquiries and was lucky enough to get an invitation from Ernie Friesen, then the Professor in charge of the American Institute of Court Management, run initially from Denver University. He ran an annual six week residential training course for court managers at Aspen in Colorado, or more accurately

Aspen-at-Snowmass. I had become friendly in 1969 with Gordon Borrie, then a professor of law at Birmingham University, and later as Sir Gordon Borrie, Director-General of Fair Trading: later still Lord Borrie, taking, methinks, the Labour whip. We had each made a mark by giving fairly hard hitting lectures for "Justice", in the Lord Chief Justices' Court of all places – my knees knocked until I got going. He spoke on small claims courts, his speciality, and true enough, they were created some six or seven years later. I spoke of crime and punishment, explaining the need for being beastly to criminals and jigging up court administration....., I got nowhere, as sentences became more sloppy, more probation officers were appointed, and crime rose at an alarming rate in direct proportion to the increase in the number of probation officers. Court administration was re-vamped, but only Crown Courts, not really an important part of my agenda. But I digress.

Gordon, like me, had not visited the U.S.A. and was keen to see their small claims courts, and meet people from the Vera Institute. And we both wanted to see the University at Berkley, across the Golden Gate bridge, at San Francisco. We got there too. It was possible for him to join me, and Ernie Friesen's organisation would pay our fares in America, a considerable financial help. I know we each bought a ticket for £100 or thereabouts, and could fly anywhere in the U.S.A. for three weeks. We did. The airlines were competing in 1970, and I suspect that we each ate and drank (wine) to a value exceeding £100, flying hither and thither. We flew

Alleghany, Frontier, Air West and several others, now
mostly merged with Big Brother airlines. We got to Aspen
by Rocky Mountain Airways (what else?) from Denver,
and saw this beautiful countryside for the first time. The
film stars get to Aspen in summer for a rest, as do a lot of
spoilt children, whose Daddies send a cheque for
maintenance each Friday – to keep the children away
from home we were told, but I thought that a bit harsh.
The hunters arrive in the fall, and shoot bear, or anything
else that gets in the way, again we were told. Come winter
and the skiers arrive, *en masse*. I saw my first "ski-in"
bank at Aspen at Snowmass. Ski up to the bank window
and cash your cheque. Those ski lifts are quite something
– and quite scary. Colleen, my wife, on a later visit, once
got fast half way up on one that broke down, swaying
madly from side to side in the wind, land 30 feet below
at a 45 degree angle with wild bear roaming. She refused
point blank to complete the last third of the journey, when
eventually freed, and hoisted to the second stage post.

   On this course on my first visit there were judges and
court administrators from most States in the U.S.A. I
actually saw the (brief!) budget papers for the New York
courts. Maybe six large binders, each four or five inches
thick. Computerised figures they were, when some U.K.
courts budgets were still typewritten or even
handwritten. But what delightful people they were, so
very kind and generous, including us in their barbecues,
social events, swimming, and so on. We each gave a
couple of lectures about the English systems of courts
and were very well received indeed. I think they were

surprised at the simplicity of our court administration. They were certainly very surprised at the lack of corruption, still current in some States. $50 to the clerk of the court to list a case even. They were incredulous that no one had ever offered me a bribe, especially in my role of assessing some lawyers defence fees. They could not understand why magistrates did the job for nothing. I did my best to explain all, and it bore some fruit, but they were clear it would not work in the dear old U.S.A. One practical exercise consisted of arguing with their paying authority for a pool table in the judges room, a luxury resisted by the authority, but demanded by the judge, really for the hours the jury were out. I didn't dare suggest he started other work whilst the jury was out. It seemed blasphemous.

I went to Aspen several times, (the pay was good) and was able to spend some time with my cousin, Jut Castleberry and his family in Claremont, California, after the seminars, or my part in them. We had last met in England in 1944, when he was stationed in Lancashire with the U.S. Air Force, and he visited my parents. Quite unexpectedly I had a few days leave while my damaged ship was being repaired in Newcastle, and we had rather a merry time, putting it mildly. We reminisced a little – when our wives were elsewhere. The first time I arrived at Los Angeles International Airport to stay with my cousin at Claremont I was leaving the main exit for the coach at the bus station outside when I was approached by a little old lady. "Excuse me young man," – my heart warmed to the Americans – "Do you know where the coach for Pasadena leaves from", "Why yes" I said "I've just travelled 6,000 miles, and I've never been here before in my life, but it's stand 4 over there." Would you believe that as she spoke, a coach showing Pasadena pulled up at stand 4. She looked at me "Thanks. I don't think you're gonna have any travel problems."

Chapter 8

Cases

In the course of a lifetime, working in courts, there are so many cases that stick in the mind. Funny, even hilarious, but mostly not to the people involved, so you need a straight face whatever happens. Tragic where death is involved, be it murder, manslaughter, infanticide or death by driving dangerously, or even carelessly driving a motor vehicle. In memories you can only list a few, or you would drive your publisher mad, or worse bore your readers.

I start with what I think was the cleverest thing I ever did. I was an articled pupil in Buxton in the early fifties, and the sole court assistant. The police sent down a weekly list of people to be prosecuted, and in the list was the name of a lady, accused of parking her car illegally on the wrong side of the road, Spring Gardens on the North Side of the High Street. To appease the shopkeepers of Spring Gardens, the authorities had come up with a sensible scheme of allowing parking on the North side on even dates, and on the South side on odd dates, the opposite side being prohibited, so the perpetual burden of parked cars outside the shop was spared. Where you could park was indicated by a sign, alternated by a hinged half circle to indicate parking prohibited that

day, or allowed. For some reason I actually looked at the
Regulations, and I now doubt any court clerk has done
that before or since, although maybe I malign them. After
checking it half a dozen times, I found that the lady could
park on the North side as the date of the alleged offence
was an even date whatever the signs said. I told the police
to drop the case, sharpish after they checked and
confirmed, and this they did. What had happened was
this. The signs on both sides of the road were changed
by dropping or raising the hinged half circle signs at 6am
daily, but the task was delegated to the council street
cleaner, always on duty at 6am. He religiously changed
the signs at 6am daily for years, as did his holiday
substitute, but no one showed them the Regulations, so,
when there were 31 days in a month, two odd days in a
row, he still carried on changing the signs. I calculated
that over 10 years the signs were wrong for three or four
years of that time. It proved impossible to go back for all
those wrongly convicted of illegal parking, but at least it
got it right for the future.

There is a delightful pub at Long Itchington in
Warwickshire, within the bailiwick of Southam magistrates' court. At the front of the pub was a large car-park,
where the cars could be parked in half a dozen rows, in
echelon. In private practice then, about 1958, I was
consulted by a very chastened motorist, who showed me
his summons to court for careless driving and failing to
stop after an accident. Would I represent him at court,
and plead guilty? He was extremely contrite, and was so
ashamed of his behaviour that he could not face the court,

if it could be done in his absence. No problem, but what had he done? He told me. He had drunk to excess in the pub, eight or nine pints, and unwisely thought he could drive home, a few miles away. His motor car was in the pub car-park near the pub door, so he drove down the alleyway between the other echelon parked cars and, alas, he hit five of them, on the right, the left, the right, the left, and right again, *seriatim* as they say. The owners of those vehicles, and others there, did not appreciate this piece of driving as they were leaving the pub at the same, closing, time. My client could remember angry shouts behind him, and saw more than one clenched fist being waved at him. He drove on and home somehow, but the "victims" got his car number, and told the local police. Today, virtually instantaneously, the police could get the name and address of the owner of the car via the computer. But then there was no computer, and the police could only get to him after the local taxation office opened at 9am the next day: by which time he was quite sober. The police arrived at his home later the day after, as expected, but any chance of a charge of drunk driving had gone. He admitted his bad driving and he was told that he would hear more. He did and the summonses which followed he showed me. He was not poor, and indicated that whatever damage had been caused to other cars would be put right and paid for by him, and I recall he did later pay up as he said.

But there was a snag. If he could be charged with drunk driving, as it was then before Breathalysers, the driving could take place on a road or public place, which the car park probably was. But careless driving and failing to stop after an accident had to take place on a road, which the car park certainly was not. I ought to take the point in court, to lead to an acquittal, but did he want me to? He wrestled with his conscience – he really wanted to be punished (he was later methinks by my bill) -but common sense prevailed and I was to take the technical point in court, without his attendance. I told the police they could stop witnesses, but the plea would be not guilty, and they knew straight away why. They had tried it on and lost. I duly appeared at Southam court, and explained the public place/road point and with some reluctance, after a retirement, both charges were dismissed. Now the crunch point. I applied for costs against the police, but failed miserably. Today the costs would be awarded automatically, but there was more discretion then for the court. But it was a blatant "try on" by the police, albeit brought on by the motorists abject admission to them of his bad behaviour. I suspect that he told them that he would plead guilty to anything. None of the solicitors who appeared at Southam ever got costs against the police, or so they said, and several of us younger ones decided that when we did we would produce a tie with the near Warwickshire police crest on, with crossed pound notes underneath the initials S.M.C. for Southam magistrates court. To be worn by those winning the costs battle only! The tie was never produced I am sad to say.

The *Christine Marie* was a fascinating case brought by Ag. and Fish, against the French owner of the boat.

She was caught fishing in "our" waters, but lawfully there as a consequence of Sir Edward Heath's gift of our fishing rights to the Europeans. There were rules at the time about the size of fishing nets, so calculated (by someone, somewhere) that young (small) fish would not be trapped, and thus left to breed, preserving fish stocks. Fishermen are nothing if not adventurous, and some had devised and used a second net, trailing, which aborted the original aim. The European Commission in Brussels had a look at this and decided that these second nets were unlawful and were to be forbidden. As an afterthought it was decided there would be some exceptions to this, to be decided later. But between then and the arrest of the *Christine Marie* some two or three years later, no such exceptions had been promulgated and the commission is still arguing about them for all I know.

The defence admitted the second net, but said it was there merely to protect the main net dragging on the sea bed, and becoming damaged: truly nets are expensive equipment. It was urged that this might well have been an exception if Brussels had got round to them. It was not a bad argument. The plea to fishing with the second net had been not guilty, and it appeared to me, and then the magistrates, that it wasn't right to convict if there was even a "might be" defence. Those exceptions should have been in place so fishermen (even foreign ones, who would probably disregard them anyway) knew where they were. If Europe didn't know, how could the fishermen know? Impasse.

At the time, (about 1975), I think only one other case had ever been referred to the European Court by a British court. But ever adventurous, as the fishermen, the case was referred by the bench to the European Court in Luxembourg for clarification of the position.

Ag. and Fish did not like this at all and took immediate proceedings in the High Court, to have the reference quashed. I think it was by Judicial Review, but it could have been Case Stated, I forget. No matter, the High Court looked at it a year or so later, and came to the conclusion that whilst a magistrates court should not normally refer a case to the European Court direct, local appeals going first, this was a case, on its facts, which merited the reference. Ag. and Fish retired, bloody, but unbowed, and the appeal case found its way into the law reports.

And so to the European Court in Luxembourg. There were no rules then about what papers to send to Luxembourg, so I treated it as a case stated and set out the facts, and tried to apply the law, but of course I couldn't, no one knew what it was, or would be. I posed the dilemma. This appeared to satisfy Luxembourg who acknowledged with thanks. And then the hearing in Luxembourg came some two and a half years after the original hearing. I thought I ought to be there to hear this momentous occasion, and a grateful state paid my fare and hotel bill. Even my fare back.

Submissions had been made in advance in writing by the parties, and the three judges allowed each advocate about 30 minutes of oral argument. These were for the defence, Ag. and Fish, and I think the Foreign Office. The Judges agreed English as the language for the hearing. Well, it was all too easy for the European Court. In a situation like this the home court should make a decision, even if there were gaps in the law. Importantly the home court should try to comply with the spirit of what the European law was getting at, and fill the gaps themselves. So we got it back again, surrounded by these words of wisdom. Lord Denning was pleased, it followed his own views, and so was I. It was a good trip, made better the day after the court hearing when I saw Luxembourg play Hungary in Luxembourg in a soccer world cup qualifier. I even saw the famous Puskas, then the Hungarian coach. Hungary won, and I suppose Europe did.

Every so often you get an unexpected situation and result, sometimes pleasant. It was a domestic court in Plymouth, and we got started on what looked like being a very bitter husband and wife dispute. The court decided to adjourn for 10 minutes, for some reason, maybe tea, and the magistrates left the room. I was going to join them, and really almost without thinking, I turned to the husband and said "I think you should buy her a cup of tea, you've both been waiting an hour or more, and she looks tired". I left the room. The court reassembled 10 minutes on, and to my amazement the husband stood up and said "When you adjourned, the clerk suggested I bought my wife a cup of tea; I did and we started talking about our affairs: as a result we are not proceeding with this case and we are going home together, to make a fresh start. We are grateful for the suggestion of tea." Well, some you win.

Chapter 9

In *Futuro*

I often get asked, in retirement, where our criminal justice system went wrong and what can be done to improve it. I have never changed my views much, over the years – indeed many views have hardened.

Winston Churchill once said in WW2, of a situation in North Africa, that the position was serious, but not hopeless. The criminal justice system now, in my view is hopeless, but not serious. This is because the courts can only ever be a gesture by society. Most criminals are not caught, and when they are, many are wrongly acquitted. If sentenced the sentence is often inadequate.

The rot really set in when Roy Jenkins was Home Secretary with his so called civilised society. Ted Heath is as bad with an outlook just as woolly, certainly with regard to Europe and they have done immense damage to us all, as even a quick look at our criminal statistics and economics show. There was a time when I took an immediate contrary opinion to anything Mr. Heath put forward, on the basis that if he proposed it, then it must be wrong.

I am asked what needs to be done, but I fear that there is little chance of much being achieved, the way our politicians and Parliament are. But if I were the

Obergrüpenführer then – that is a different affair. Oh to be Obergrüpenführer.

Probation I would halve the present number of probation officers, by wastage, over perhaps five years. Abolish the need for courts to have probation reports by virtual compulsion, and leave the courts to ask if they thought one helpful and needed in sentencing. Prohibit any probation officer from giving his/her opinion on sentence. I have seen some dreadful suggestions in my time. The victim nearly dead and a conditional discharge put forward. Take all probation officers out of prison (unless in on a lawful sentence), get the social workers out of the juvenile courts, which have been turned into a powerless laughing stock almost, partly by silly legislation and partly by social worker involvement. I can remember care cases in the juvenile courts where the parties comprised the Children's Officer, bringing the case, Mum (when Dad had disappeared) the child and that was it. You are lucky to get into court today, so crowded is it, and the parties comprise, the social worker, the child, Mum, (Dad still gone) a guardian *ad litem* (another social worker but independent albeit employed by the local county council), grandma/grandpa, and all, but all, represented by a solicitor. I know which decisions were better, between 1949 and 1989 – 1949 wins hands down.

Legal Aid This is surely abused. It is said, in early 1997 that a serious fraud office case at the Crown Court, brought a defence lawyer's bill of £4 million. If that is so, it confirms my view that some defence lawyers are writing their own cheques. To stop that, cap all defence costs at £1 million, and a court should review, monthly, every bill approaching £½ million. For run of the mill cases, with a guilty plea (80%), there really is little need for lawyers attendance to give mitigation only. Some days in court I despaired, hearing exactly the same mitigation several times in one morning. I came up with a scheme for the advocate to say a number, only, and sit down.

ONE   = He's sorry

TWO   = He's sorry and his girl friend is pregnant

THREE = He's sorry, his girlfriend is pregnant, and he has a job to go to on Monday

FOUR   = He's sorry, his girl friend is pregnant, he has a job to go to on Monday, and I ask you to sentence in accordance with the probation officers recommendation in his report on page 15, paragraph 57.

FIVE   = Perhaps the court would consider an absolute or conditional discharge, but if not a further short period of probation would assist the offender. However a small fine would be a punishment, and could be paid weekly at £2 from his social security money. If not, he could put something back into the community by some community service, which he is willing to do, even though it failed last time. The court will not be thinking of imprisonment, of course, as the jails are so overcrowded, so any possible imprisonment would need to be suspended and it would be a hold over him. Any imprisonment to be served (Heaven forbid) should only be for a month or so, so as not to be an embarrassment to his family who will have to remain on social security.

But it never took off for some reason.

I think mitigation is better put by the written word, not by an advocate pleading in court in many cases. This would only follow in comparatively minor cases, minor thefts and the like, after free legal aid advice on the plea, subject to means. The mitigation by solicitors letter would be read out in open court. All this would save vast sums of money, but the lawyers would need to be (over) paid for the advice and mitigation letter. The congestion at courts (and nearby car parks) at about 10am would be relieved enormously. Legal Aid and representation by advocate should be freely available to any accused facing any request by a prosecutor for remand in custody. It is the run of the mill guilty plea in comparatively minor cases I am getting at, the great majority of cases in court. In not guilty cases, the minority, advocates need to be freely available.

Court Administration I would decree a return of part-time justices' clerks (local solicitors/barristers) for any town in the population range 50,000 – 100,000, if the magistrates there wanted it. Magistrates' courts' committees should be abolished overnight leaving the Lord Chancellor to make any administrative decisions, and finance the courts. He has to approve any decision of substance by the magistrates' courts' committee anyway, so it simply cuts out the middleman, and puts magistrates' courts on a par with Crown and County courts. In matters of substance, say the appointment of a new justices' clerk, or a new court house, the Chairman of the Bench/es and his deputy/ies could advise the Lord Chancellor who would have the final word, as he does now. It is a fact that most magistrates' courts are just about self financing, if not run at a profit, as the fines collected equal court administration costs, in round figures.

Magistrates I cannot see the European Union allowing our system of lay magistrates to continue when they get round to it, assuming that we stay in the European Union. All Europe has career judges and we shall be made to fall into line.

I say that advisedly, as the first steps have already been taken, albeit in a secretive way, so often the practice of the European Union. The press were not informed, or invited, and thus did not report. In April 1979, in San Sebastian which I know quite well, the XX Directorate General (Financial Control) held a seminar on the protection of the financial interests of the E.U., and came up with *Corpus Juris*.

The short point of *Corpus Juris* is to create a judicial machine to deal with fraud against the E.U. budget, but many attending were convinced the real purpose was to establish a Federal European Criminal Justice System. The President of the European Parliament virtually said that in his message to the seminar. One of the Articles of *Corpus Juris* declares these fraud cases should be tried by national courts, consisting of professional judges and not jurors or lay magistrates. So there you have it. The

European Union financed the full hotel and travelling expenses of some 100 lawyers from member states.

I suspect that the recent decision by the Lord Chancellor to appoint one or more Stipendiary Magistrates in all the major cities and shire counties is to pre-empt the European attack when it comes, as come it will. It also gives a springboard to appoint more stipendiaries, in a phasing in job, to replace most lay magistrates. But as we still have lay magistrates the appointing system works pretty well albeit with too much interviewing. The best magistrates are often those people who have been known to one or more members of the Advisory Committee for 20 or 30 years, at school together, that sort of thing. If it does self-perpetuate a social group, then so be it, but it cuts out the "unknown" candidate with a hidden, possibly covered up, background. It was a former Lord Chancellor who said, insultingly, that one third of the magistracy was brilliant, better than society could expect, another third was quite adequate, and the last third should never have been appointed in the first place.

There are some magistrates, it is true, who will never achieve the right judicial attitude or approach to court affairs, however much training they receive. I would simply make all appointments for five years in the first place, with a review then by the Advisory Committee to see if they should continue or not. And then to make the retirement age from the Bench 65, and not 70 as now. We all age differently, and if you cease paid work at 65 (or 60 for civil servants) judging others could also usefully cease. It avoids any embarrassment in deciding whether the 68 year old is ga-ga, or going that way, or not.

Crown Prosecutors (CPS) I would abolish the national and regional bodies. The Labour Party, just before the 1997 election, came out with a devastating attack on the CPS, the only party to do so to my knowledge. They were working on the right lines. It is simply a waste of resources to have every case pass through the CPS, and the evidence shows they are no better at making a decision to prosecute, or not, than an experienced police officer in the Chief Inspector/Superintendent bracket. So I would return the decision to prosecute or not to the police. Guilty plea cases, run of the mill, could be handled in court by a senior police officer, as they were for a hundred years. Not Guilty cases should have lawyers on both sides, but whether the prosecution used an "inhouse" tame lawyer, or went to a private practice lawyer would be up to the police. A choice.

Prisons and Sentencing Much has been done in the last two decades to remove the primitive conditions, slopping out and so on, in the older establishments. The food has improved dramatically. The building programme is moving ahead, but it all takes time. I suspect that the administration outside prisons, regional offices and so on, is top heavy, and needs thinning out leaving more decisions to prison governors. I would re-create the Prison Commissioners, who would report direct to the Home Secretary/Parliament. It gets the Home Secretary off the hook. The government should honour all requests from the Commissioners, regardless of cost, unless there was good reason not to, specified publicly in writing. The prison officers themselves are less militant than yesteryear, and I would reward them by appointing more of them: I would say they are somewhat understaffed, the financial cuts going just too far. An emphasis on appointments from the armed services would not go amiss, at the bottom, but especially at Assistant Governor level. The trendy young graduate Assistant Governor would be out for me, and in would come the retired major or Colonel. If a prisoner has lost his liberty by lawful sentence, it seems odd that he has not lost his civil rights, like voting at elections. I would remedy that. Mr. Howard as Home Secretary, has done a difficult job with some success. He must be right about minimum sentences, to defeat the judges who regularly under sentence. Their names are well known on the Court circuits and in various localities. I would get the Lord Chancellor to review the conduct of those under performers. The honesty in sentencing policy must also be good. If a court says two years jail, it means two years jail, not one year with automatic (that's what it is) remission of half. Judges will soon get the hang of it if they try. This proposal falls short by one simple point. If two years means two years, then any judicial disciplinary hearing of bad behaviour should be able to increase the sentence by up to half. Yes, and simply administratively.

The Police Not much wrong with the personnel, and we still have the best police forces in the world. There may well be the occasional corrupt or bent copper, but they are 99% plus dead honest. It surprises me how honest

they are, given the temptation before them, and the weak
agencies surrounding them, Home Office, Parliament and
the rest. The percentage corrupt is well below that for
lawyers, doctors, and Members of Parliament. The
problem is the number of police forces, 43 only, leading
towards a national force unless stopped. It was reduced
to this number to accommodate the Home Office officials,
who only have 43 Chief Constables to "order about". That
43 should be increased to about 100, and the need for
change by increase stands out a mile. Birmingham for
example, needs its own force, the existing West Midlands
being far too big and unwieldy to handle. Devon and
Cornwall police, should be divided into a Devon force,
and a Cornwall force, much to the pleasure of Cornwall.
John Alderson, when he was Chief Constable of Devon
and Cornwall, used to point out that his headquarters at
Exeter was nearer to London than Penzance in the West,
far too large a geographical area. There is no mileage in
the argument that these immense forces create economy
of scale. Even if they did, the improvement in morale by
belonging to the smaller unit would outweigh it.
Technology is so advanced that large scale economy
hardly matters.